Cybersecurity for Space

Protecting the Final Frontier

Jacob G. Oakley

Apress®

Cybersecurity for Space: Protecting the Final Frontier

Jacob G. Oakley
Owens Cross Roads, AL, USA

ISBN-13 (pbk): 978-1-4842-5731-9   ISBN-13 (electronic): 978-1-4842-5732-6
https://doi.org/10.1007/978-1-4842-5732-6

Managing Director, Apress Media LLC: Welmoed Spahr
Acquisitions Editor: Susan McDermott
Development Editor: Laura Berendson
Coordinating Editor: Rita Fernando

Cover designed by eStudioCalamar

Cover image designed by Freepik (www.freepik.com)

Distributed to the book trade worldwide by Springer Science+Business Media New York, 1 New York Plaza, New York, NY 10004. Phone 1-800-SPRINGER, fax (201) 348-4505, e-mail orders-ny@springer-sbm.com, or visit www.springeronline.com. Apress Media, LLC is a California LLC and the sole member (owner) is Springer Science + Business Media Finance Inc (SSBM Finance Inc). SSBM Finance Inc is a **Delaware** corporation.

For information on translations, please e-mail rights@apress.com, or visit http://www.apress.com/rights-permissions.

Apress titles may be purchased in bulk for academic, corporate, or promotional use. eBook versions and licenses are also available for most titles. For more information, reference our Print and eBook Bulk Sales web page at http://www.apress.com/bulk-sales.

Any source code or other supplementary material referenced by the author in this book is available to readers on GitHub via the book's product page, located at www.apress.com/9781484257319. For more detailed information, please visit http://www.apress.com/source-code.

Printed on acid-free paper

To my children,

If a crayon-eating Marine can get published writing a book about hacking computers in outer space, you can accomplish anything.

Table of Contents

About the Author

Dr. Jacob G. Oakley spent over seven years in the US Marines originally involved in satellite communications and later was one of the founding members in the operational arm of the Marine Corps Forces Cyberspace Command. After his enlistment, he wrote and taught an advanced computer operations course, eventually returning back to mission support. He left government contracting to do threat emulation and red teaming at a private company for commercial clients, serving as the principal penetration tester and director of penetration testing and cyber operations. He is currently working as a cybersecurity subject matter expert for a government customer, advising on cybersecurity integration and strategy. He completed his doctorate in IT at Towson University, researching and developing offensive cybersecurity methods, and is the author of *Professional Red Teaming: Conducting Successful Cybersecurity Engagements* (Apress, 2019) as well as *Waging Cyber War: Technical Challenges and Operational Constraints* (Apress, 2019).

About the Technical Reviewer

Dr. Albert B. Bosse is a practicing spacecraft engineer, currently serving as chief engineer for electro-optical and infrared space vehicles for a government customer. He has over 28 years of experience applying his expertise in aerospace vehicle structures, structural dynamics, guidance, navigation and control, and systems engineering for the advancement of tactical intelligence, surveillance, and reconnaissance capabilities within the U.S. Department of Defense. His notable past positions include Spacecraft Control Systems Branch Head at the Naval Research Laboratory (2001–2005), Associate Professor of Aerospace Engineering at the University of Cincinnati (2005–2008), Technical Director of the Missile Defense Agency Interceptor Knowledge Center (2009–2017), and Chief Scientist of the Missile Defense Agency Ground-Based Midcourse Defense Program (2019). The organizations he previously served include the Naval Research Laboratory, Swales Aerospace, Draper Laboratory, and the Johns Hopkins University Applied Physics Lab.

Dr. Bosse earned M.S. and Ph.D. in aerospace engineering from the University of Cincinnati in 1991 and 1993, respectively, as well as a B.S. in physics from Thomas More University in 1987.

Acknowledgments

I would like to thank my beautiful wife and family for putting up with this and other nerdy endeavors.

To Dr. Al Bosse who performed the technical review for this book and has been a font of knowledge about space and space vehicle operations, this book would not be possible without you.

To all you keyboard-wielding cyber warriors out there protecting freedom, I salute you.

Introduction

As a cybersecurity professional, the more I learn about space systems, the more I realize how underprepared the space industry is against cybersecurity threats and how unaware the cybersecurity industry is of the space domain in general. I wrote this book to provide a primer on space systems and the concepts of space vehicle operations to cybersecurity practitioners. The environmental and operational challenges and constraints faced by space systems are considerable. The threats and vectors by which those threats will affect space systems are imposed or created by these challenges and constraints. After reading this book, cybersecurity professionals will have the building blocks of knowledge necessary to develop and implement solutions to space system issues which not only improve the resiliency and security of those systems but allow them or enable them to conduct their mission. I also provide macro- and microanalysis of compromise scenarios involving space systems to drive home the very real and present risk to such systems via the cyber domain. Though written from the perspective of and for the primary audience of the cybersecurity industry, space domain operators, designers, and developers can surely benefit from understanding the threats, vectors, and issues that cyber brings with it. This is especially relevant given the interconnectivity and continued digitization and software definition of space system components.

CHAPTER 1

Space Systems

Before I get into the specifics of space systems, I just want to make clear that this book is written with cybersecurity professionals in mind and by a cybersecurity professional. That is not to say that those who design and operate space vehicles (SVs) or the generally curious have nothing to gain from reading it. Quite the opposite in fact. This book is written with the intent of priming the cybersecurity community on the intricacies of space systems, their high difficulty and risk during operation, as well as the distinct challenges of security in outer space.

As such, there will be descriptions, illustrations, and scenarios involving space systems and their operation that will be at times simplified and potentially unrealistic. I am trying to educate the security perspective on the difficult task ahead regarding creating and implementing solutions to protect systems in space. Any space topics are covered only to the extent necessary to aid in that understanding. There is plenty of literature regarding designing and operating systems to fly in outer space, and if that topic interests you, as it does openly or secretly all nerds, I encourage you to read up on the fascinating subject. This book is my attempt to address what I feel is a gap in the cybersecurity community's awareness for the growing presence of computers in outer space and a lack of comprehension for the implications of space operations on cybersecurity.

Tipping Point

We are currently at a precarious position in the evolution and accessibility of space operations to academic, commercial, and government entities. More and more computing platforms are being launched into orbit and beyond. Unfortunately, these systems, as a necessity, have a heavy focus on functionality, and any regard to cybersecurity is oftentimes a byproduct of attempts at safeguarding the space system from failure and not any malicious intent. This means that we are revisiting an era in computing where the operators and any operation passed to the device are trusted; after

1

© Jacob G. Oakley 2020
J. G. Oakley, *Cybersecurity for Space*, https://doi.org/10.1007/978-1-4842-5732-6_1

all, why would I do anything to damage my multimillion-dollar satellite program? Why would someone do that?

The problem is that plenty of people would do that, from hacktivists, cybercriminals, and nation state actors to commercial competitors engaging in industrial espionage. Exacerbating this potential nasty situation is the fact that everything is becoming increasingly connected; after all, why wouldn't you want to check the status of your SV with a smart phone application? How else are you going to show off your space program to fellow academics or sell the accessibility of your space system to potential customers in the commercial world?

It is not hard to imagine that a large percentage of space operations moving forward will be inherently accessible for one reason or another to some system or systems on the Internet. Even if not, recent history is littered with examples of malicious code that has allowed the spread and infection of cyber attack effects across devices connected not to the Internet or even any other network at all.

Worst of all, the computational resources available to any would-be attacker are immense when compared to the available resources on a space system that could be dedicated in some way to cybersecurity. As we will cover more in depth later, once a malicious actor gains access to the computer on the ground that communicates with a space system, there is almost implicit trust and no further defense in depth for the space system or systems that communicate with that terrestrial computer.

An Introduction to Space Systems

The most basic example of a space system is where there is a device on the ground transmitting to and/or receiving from a device in space that is transmitting and/or receiving. For the purpose of this book, we will refer to the device on the ground that transmits and/or receives as the "ground station" and will refer to the device in space that transmits or receives as the "SV." Often nowadays, the ground station is where the SV is flown from—although it has not always been the case and will not always be the case that the SV is flown. For instance, if we go back to one of the most famous space systems, the Sputnik 1 satellite, it had no way of flying at all. It was shot into orbit and flew around the Earth with no ability for steering. In fact, it did not receive any instructions from a ground station at all, it just broadcast a radio wave signal that could be heard by anyone on Earth with a radio antenna tuned to the correct frequency.

This is a far cry from some of the extremely complex systems of today. Consider the International Space Station (ISS). It regularly makes maneuvers using onboard propulsion to move out of the way of space debris that is on a collision path with it. In the case of the ISS, it can be flown from on board the station itself as well as by individuals at a ground station on Earth. The orbital planes of the Earth are inhabited by SVs spanning the full spectrum of sophistication from derelict or antiquated satellites to complex constellations of multifunctional SVs. The simple example of one SV and one ground station is shown in Figure 1-1.

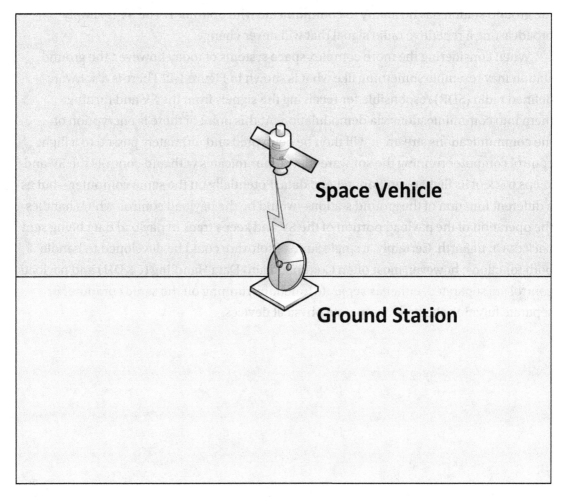

Space Vehicle

Ground Station

Figure 1-1. *Basic Space System*

The Ground Station Design

As you might imagine, ground stations come in varying shapes and sizes and levels of complexity. In the case of the Sputnik 1 space system, any home radio essentially operated as a ground station, receiving the beeping signal as the satellite flew overhead. The SV had no other functionality than to emit this beep, and all a ground station had to do for the mission of Sputnik 1 to be successful was for amateur radio operators on the ground to hear it via their radio ground stations. In the Sputnik 1 example, we would not say that the SV is actually communicating with the ground station, and certainly the ground station has no ability to communicate with Sputnik 1. The SV is simply broadcasting a repetitive radio signal that will never change.

When considering the more complex space systems of today however, the ground station may resemble something like what is shown in Figure 1-2. There is a software defined radio (SDR) responsible for receiving the signals from the SV and turning them into communications via demodulation. At this point, if there is encryption of the communications stream, it will then be decrypted and ultimately passed to a flight control computer running the software that communicates with and controls the SV and keeps track of its flight operation–related data. Potentially on the same computer—but as a different function of the ground station—would be the payload control, which handles the operation of the payload portion of the SV and keeps track of payload data being sent back down to Earth. Certainly, a single suite of software could be developed to handle both functions; however, most often Command and Data Handling (C&DH) and payload control are separated, either as separate functions running on the same computer or separate functions hosted on separate physical devices.

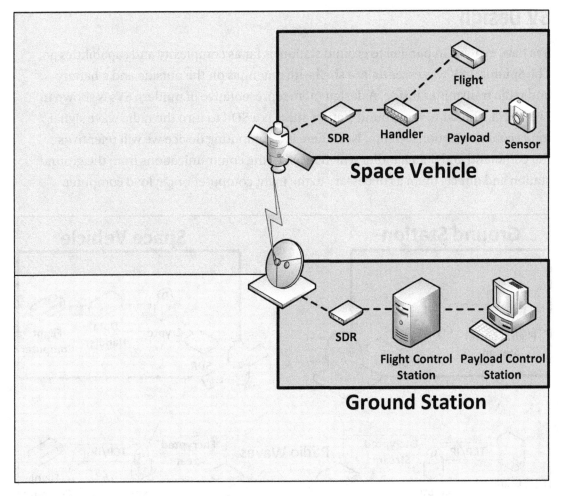

Figure 1-2. *Detailed Space System View*

One other facet of the ground station that I will not cover in great detail at this point is the antenna itself. This is the dish or other type of antennas that allows the SDR to receive the signal wave from the air and/or transmit it back to the SV. The process from the ground station perspective is just the opposite, where a communications stream is crafted using a protocol like, or in actuality, the Internet Protocol (IP) and then encrypted if necessary, then modulated and sent as a radio wave via the SDR and antennas into the air to the SV.

SV Design

SVs have evolved in parallel to ground station as far as complexity and capabilities go. The Sputnik 1 SV was essentially a shell with antennas on the outside and a battery and radio transmitter inside. A design more representative of modern SVs is shown in Figure 1-3. Similar to the ground station, there is a SDR to turn the radio wave signal into a communications stream. Next there is a computing device we will refer to as the command and data handler which receives the communications from the ground station and directs them as necessary to the flight computer or payload computer.

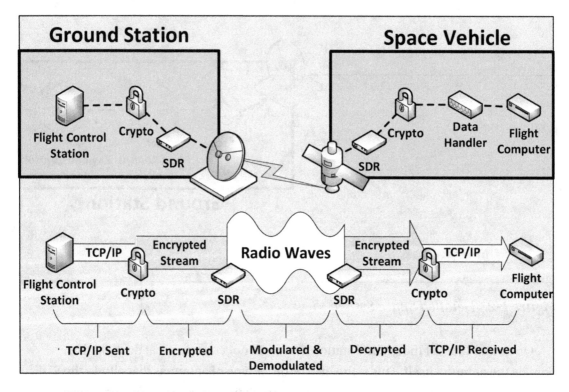

Figure 1-3. *Communications Process*

The flight computer is responsible for controlling the functions of the SV with regard to flight. What those functions are will be covered in the upcoming section on SV functions. The payload control computer is responsible for manipulating the payload of the SV. A payload is the portion of the SV carrying out the mission it was designed for. As an example of a payload, Figure 1-2 shows a camera. The payload computer would be responsible for telling the camera when to snap pictures, as well as storing those pictures and their metadata for later transmission to the ground.

Ground Station Functionality

Simply stated, the required functionality of the ground station is to communicate with the SV. Doing so requires the performance of several other tasks that we need to understand. Depending on the type of communication needed, the ground station may either have a stationary, nondirectional antenna or a movable directional antenna. With the radio signal from Sputnik 1, the waves were emitted by the SV in all directions, and therefore there were no directional requirements for the receipt of that signal by all the home radio antennas that had been tuned to the correct frequency.

The same can be said for modern-day satellite radio, that the receiving ground station has no need to directionally track the SV it is receiving signals from to do its geosynchronous orbit (more on this later). Using the example of our ground station in Figure 1-2 however, we are using a directional antenna to communicate with the SV which must slew the antenna in line with the passing SV and with more agility required as the orbit altitude of that SV decreases. With directional communications, we are talking to the SV by pointing the ground station transmitter receiver in line with the antenna on the SV which will do the same. This lets us utilize frequencies capable of higher bandwidth to take advantage of each time the satellite comes into view in the sky, also known as a pass (see Figure 1-4). To maintain directionality with the SV during the pass, we will need the ground station antenna to move in lock with the orbiting SV.

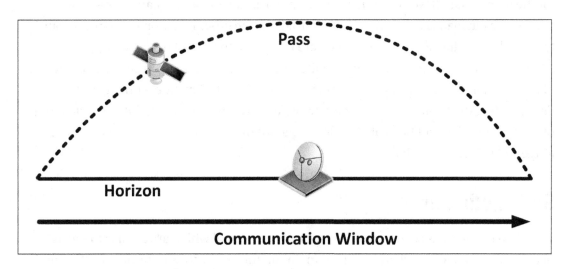

Figure 1-4. *Diagram of a Pass*

Communication with a SV moving relative to the Earth's surface requires more than an ability for the ground station to move its antenna and take advantage of the full pass for a longer communication window. It also requires that the ground station have a really good idea of where the SV will start its pass so that it can already be facing the correct location on the horizon and not waste time spinning the antenna around. This situation becomes much more complex if you have a single ground station that will communicate with multiple satellites, since instead of simply waiting for one satellite to come over the horizon, it will have to address and deconflict multiple orbits.

Ground stations communicate with SVs in several ways, which we have already partially covered. In newer and complex systems, there is a need for both receiving and transmission of signals and ultimately communications. Depending on the configuration and capabilities of the SV, this may require the ground station to have an ability to not only transmit and receive but potentially do both simultaneously. In some instances, communications windows where a SV is in view of a ground station can be very short. In order to receive communications and thus tasking of the vehicle or downlinking of data from the vehicle to the ground, bidirectional communications make space operations much more efficient, though they do make the SV and ground station more complex.

This gets us into the other complex function of ground stations, tasking. The ground station is the interface between the humans using the SV and the vehicle itself. There are essentially two types of tasking. There are tasks for the SV flight and there are tasks for the SV payload. If we continue the example of a satellite with a camera payload, tasking the payload is pretty straightforward. I use the ground station to communicate tasks to the satellite about when and where to take pictures. As far as tasking the SV itself goes, I might need to task the satellite to alter its orbit slightly to get a better picture of a particular area of interest. I also might need to task the satellite with regard to downloading those pictures from the satellite or perhaps task the satellite with deleting older pictures I haven't been able to download for one reason or another, as they are no longer relevant and needed.

SV Functionality

The SV in general has several required functions, some of which are similar to those of the ground station, such as having to maintain the ability to communicate allowing it to receive tasking. It also has to be able to carry out its mission as well as maintain communications with users on the ground and stay in the correct attitude, on the correct orbit, and achieve necessary positioning. It is necessary to simultaneously satisfy these constraints to maintain communications needs, maintain SV flight requirements, and enable payload operation. The payload refers to the portion of the SV specific to carrying out its mission such as taking pictures or recording signal data. The part of the spacecraft responsible for housing and controlling everything needed for the SV to fly is known as the bus; an example of this separation is shown in Figure 1-5.

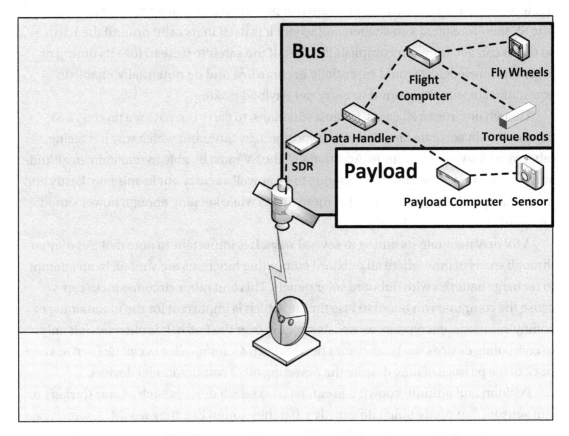

Figure 1-5. *Payload and Bus*

Maintaining communications is done in much the same manner as is handled by the ground station; the SV needs to make sure its antenna responsible for communications with the ground station is directionally oriented, when necessary, with the ground antenna. It is worth noting that phased array antennas are becoming more common in ground stations and SVs, where antennas are roughly oriented and beam control is employed by the SV to simultaneously point tens of communications beams to ground terminals located on the Earth. However, for our example, during the communications window of a pass, the SV needs to make sure it transmits and receives as necessary to offload payload and flight data as well as take on tasking. In certain instances, SVs may have a payload sensor on one end and a communication antenna on the opposite. This would mean that during passes over ground stations, the satellite would need to rotate its communication antenna toward the Earth and, after its pass, begin orienting the opposite side, with, say, a camera, back toward the Earth to carry out its tasked mission of taking a picture of a particular place at a particular time. The SV therefore must know when and where it is itself in its orbit around the Earth so that it can accurately accomplish this feat. If the satellite were to lose its timing or location knowledge, it would essentially become lost and be potentially unable to communicate with the ground or carry out payload tasking.

Though not true in all cases, in most situations, to carry out payload tasking, a SV must maintain accurate knowledge of its position, its time, and which way it is facing, otherwise known as its attitude. Additionally, the SV must be able to maintain an attitude and position that allows for it to continue to fly as well as carry out its mission. Lastly and most importantly, a SV must do all of these things while keeping enough power stored on board to continue to do so.

A SV may maintain its timing in several ways. It is important to note that SVs may go through spans of time where all onboard computing functions are shut off in an attempt to recharge batteries with onboard solar panels. This and other circumstances can cause the computers on board to lose timing, which is important for the maintaining of communications, encryption, as well as position over the Earth. It is often not left only to computing devices, and sometimes devices such as atomic clocks can be used to keep track of the passage of time despite the powering off of computational devices.

Position and attitude knowledge can be tracked via devices such as star trackers or sun sensors that pretty much do exactly what they sound like they would. A star tracker is a device that uses knowledge of specific star positions and the reading of stellar lights to identify both where the SV may be in orbit and what its attitude may be. The sun sensor is a less accurate but similar type of device that used the sensing of light from our sun and its strength to make rough determinations of location on orbit as well as general attitude.

Maintaining both attitude and position is done via several methods. On complex or larger SVs, this may be done using actual propulsion. Propulsion is the use of active force to alter the course or attitude of a SV by pushing it one way or another. Another active method for attitude and course correction or adjustment is flywheels which store up energy and use that energy to essentially spin the wheels, generating inertia and altering the movement of the SV. Lastly there are torque rods, which are passive devices that are charged with energy to increase or decrease the SVs' attraction to the Earth's electromagnetic fields or gravity, as such slowly altering the position or attitude of the SV.

Maintaining these states of the spacecraft is obviously important for its flight life span as they help determine orbits, avoid potential collisions, and enable communication with ground stations. On the other hand, knowledge and maintenance of position and attitude may also be extremely important for the carrying out of mission tasking by a payload. It doesn't do anyone any good for a satellite to maintain its orbit and avoid collision if it can't get accurate attitude during camera shots by its payload. Pictures of stars or the moon aren't going to be beneficial to a mission intent on ground observation over certain terrestrial areas of interest. Actually, it is easy to imagine certain imaging, position identifying, or signal verifying types of payload missions where knowledge of attitude and position might have to be even more accurate than when the SV is communicating with the ground.

Regardless of whether for communication, payload execution, or SV survival, the knowledge and maintenance of attitude and position as well as the operation of a payload require power. On many space vehicles, power is the most constraining attribute; after all, in space power comes from solar panels and batteries, there is no outlet to plug in to. This might mean that to preserve the operation of the SV in the long term, payload mission windows may have to be sacrificed in the short term to allow the SV to keep its solar panels facing the sun and gathering energy. It means that if a course correction is required to avoid a collision with another satellite and that maneuver drains a significant amount of power from the battery that the payload may have to stay inoperable for days, weeks, or months. It also means that in instances where power may become in issue and a ground station may not be in line of sight, the SV may have to make automated decisions on when to go into power saving or charging positions and forego communications with the ground or payload execution at all until batteries can be recharged to enable such activity.

Payload execution may not seem very power intensive when it is something as simple as snapping a picture, but onboard processing via computer processing units (CPUs), graphical processing units (GPUs), or field-programmable gate arrays (FPGAs) is often very power intensive and can even compete with communication as a top power consumer. On the other hand, a payload may be doing long windows of signal collection for a specific type of signal, which might require large amounts of receiving and writing to payload hard drives. The payload may also be an emitting payload instead of a sensing one. Where a sensing payload may listen for or monitor a signal or snap a picture, an emitting payload may itself be responsible for radiating a signal of its own which would certainly be more power intensive.

Space System Architectures

To accomplish a widening and varying array of mission sets from outer space, space systems come in vastly different architectures, enabling many types of operations. There is obviously the very straightforward one SV one ground station architecture pictured in Figure 1-3 which is essentially the same diagram as shown to illustrate the basic ground station SV concept. Here the one ground station tracks each pass of the one SV. It is important to note that despite potentially orbiting the Earth in a matter of hours, the SV will not always have an orbit that brings it within sight of the ground-based antenna.

It is common that the SV may only be able to see and communicate with ground-based users for a subset of its orbits. This is due to the fact that as the SV orbits around the Earth, the Earth itself is wobbling and spinning. Any orbit not stationary relative to the surface of the Earth will traverse across it. An example of this traversal is shown in Figure 1-6.

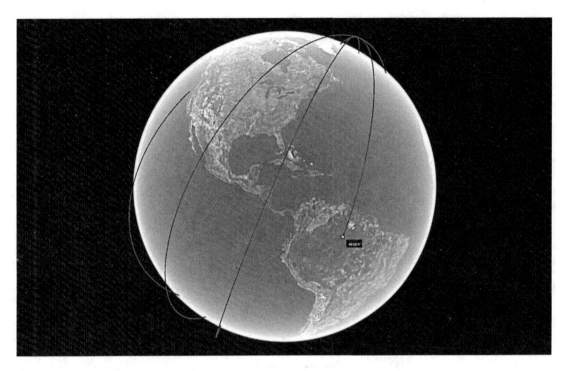

Figure 1-6. *Orbit Traversing*

Figure 1-7 shows how some architectures might take advantage of having multiple ground stations to talk to the same satellite. If these ground stations were placed at key locations around the globe, it would enable much more frequent communications windows with the SV and thus allow for more tasking as well as downloading of tasked mission data.

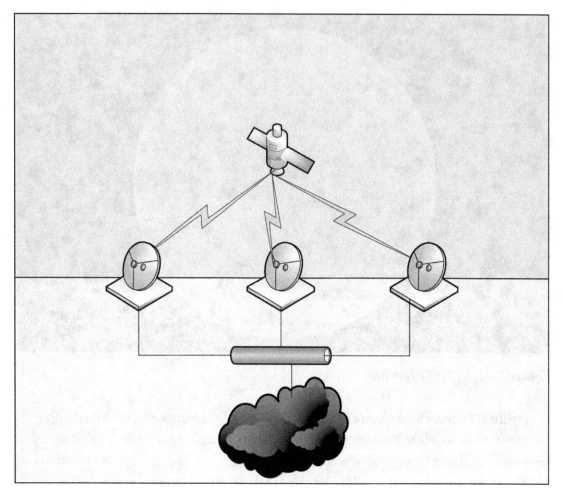

Figure 1-7. *One SV, Multiple Ground Stations*

Once the data makes it to a ground station, terrestrial networks such as the Internet can allow for users in one location to utilize all three ground stations pictured in Figure 1-8 to retrieve data from the SV and/or task it when it is overhead any of them instead of multiplying the ability to task and return data from the SV several times.

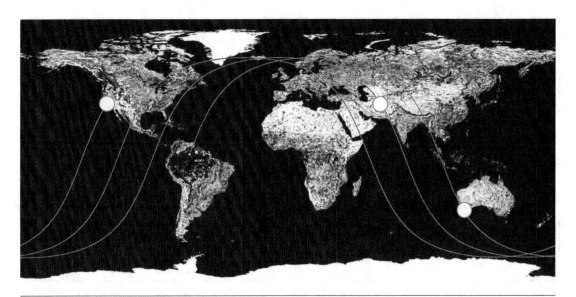

Figure 1-8. *Successive Passes*

Figure 1-8 shows how multiple ground stations at different locations might allow for the satellite to be communicated with on each of three orbits in succession. The ground station locations are represented by the circles.

Where multiple ground stations allow for more frequent communication with the SV in more places, more SVs as shown in Figure 1-9 allow for better mission coverage. By this I mean that the more SVs you have, the more likely one of them is over the area of interest for the payload to conduct its mission on, and as such, even without the improved efficiency of multiple ground stations, this space system architecture will have a higher probability of timely payload execution.

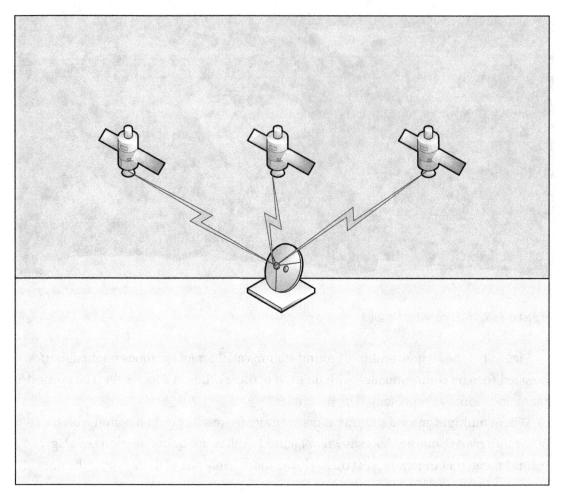

Figure 1-9. *Multiple SVs and One Ground Station*

As shown in Figure 1-10, there are also architectures for space systems that utilize the operations of multiple SVs and multiple ground stations. This further improves the ability for the space system architecture overall to have more efficient tasking and downloading as well as more efficient mission coverage.

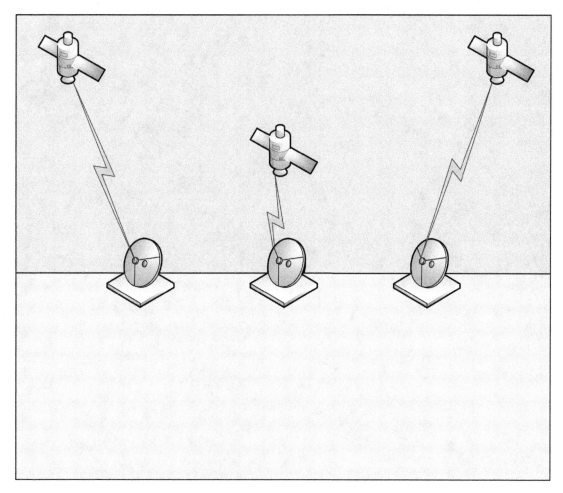

Figure 1-10. *Multiple SVs and Multiple Ground Stations*

Conclusion

This chapter has been an introduction to the rudimentary concepts of space systems and their basic components of ground stations and SVs. We covered how both the ground station and SV are actually comprised of multiple systems and that space systems themselves are systems comprised of systems of systems. The various basic architectures of space systems were covered and how multiple ground stations, SVs, or both impact space system operations. These space systems concepts and others that will be explored in the coming chapters will prepare the reader to frame cybersecurity challenges and solutions within the constraints and unique challenges of space operations.

CHAPTER 2

Space Challenges

In case it is not already starting to hit home, outer space presents an extremely complex and challenging domain within which to operate. These challenges are presented by both the environment that space vehicles (SVs) operate within and the operation of those systems themselves. The challenges of space systems are both constraints to be mitigated and dealt with and obstacles to be addressed and overcome. Even before we begin discussing malicious intent and potential adversarial actions against space systems from the cyber domain, we must first understand the risks and hardships that must be overcome by space systems in general.

Having been around the space community, to include operationally minded individuals and developmental ones, there is an onus on mission accomplishment. The SV needs to get into space, function for the window it was intended to, or longer, and communicate back these details to a ground station. It is safe to say at the writing of this book in late 2019 that the preponderance of issues faced in space systems development and operation would not include cyber-related issues beyond encryption, despite the growing prevalence of computational resources on board.

As it turns out, getting complete mission accomplishment out of a space system is extremely difficult due to the challenges of the space domain. When there is an unknown chance that a solar flare can wipe out your SV, or the launch vehicle blows up on the launch pad, trying to make time and effort for cybersecurity concerns is probably pretty far down the list of priorities. In writing this book and speaking about this topic, I am trying to inform the cybersecurity community that before long, the space community will permeate a larger and growing presence in commercial, academic, and government sectors. As this happens and as organizations get better and more efficient at operating within the space domain, we will quickly find ourselves behind the power curve, if we are not already, in being prepared to address cybersecurity threats faced by space systems in ways which work within the bounds and around the obstacles of space operations.

© Jacob G. Oakley 2020
J. G. Oakley, *Cybersecurity for Space*, https://doi.org/10.1007/978-1-4842-5732-6_2

Before we begin suggesting or implementing cybersecurity solutions, we need to make sure we understand where our solutions fall within the overall risk matrix of space operations so that solutions are not only adequate to the risk they are trying to mitigate but that they are designed in a way that the space community can easily integrate them within their systems. If we wait for the space community to come calling because a university satellite got hacked and a multiyear, multimillion-dollar academic effort was scuttled by a hacker and burned up in the atmosphere, we will be far too late. If we are honest, if that wake-up call was just an academic experiment, it would be the best-case scenario when compared to potential implications if it was a government or commercial target. Before we get to the scary possibilities of hacking SVs, we will go through the challenges of space that are faced by nearly all types of SVs.

Environmental Challenges

Environmental challenges are those that are simply inherent to operating part of a system in the space domain. For our space systems, there is at least one SV subject to the dangers of outer space. Though we will explore the unique aspects that relate to systems in terrestrial orbit around the Earth compared to other types of space systems later, the following apply to the majority of SVs regardless of orbit or function. These environmental challenges are not a complete or comprehensive list, but include some of the more impactful in general and those specifically relevant to the onboard electrical components like computers.

Radiation

Whether in the higher reaches of what is considered the Earth's atmosphere or wholly outside of it, radiation is a much more important consideration and challenge to operation than would be faced by any Earthbound system. There are various types and sources of radiation out in space, and I will certainly not cover them all in this book as they are not particularly relevant to the cybersecurity professional. On the other hand, the fact that the electrical systems that allow a SV to operate are subject to higher amounts of radiation does affect their operation. Computers communicate in 1s and 0s at the most basic level, and those 1s and 0s are on and off switches of electricity. It is pretty straightforward to see how high doses of radiation energy could hamper or destroy electrical systems operating on finely tuned flips of an on/off switch.

SVs are subjected to radiation in two fashions and with differing degrees of severity and impact. There is the more easily planned for and understood buildup of radiation absorption by the SV simply due to the radiation emitted by our sun and other distant stars at a constant rate called total ionizing dose (TID). Day-to-day and early on, the effects of this are negligible; however, the long-term exposure to such radiation can cause the functionality and accuracy of electrical computing actions to become degraded. The other type of radiation exposure is that from significant events, for example, proton flux, which may in a single exposure present more threat to the SV than the duration of radiation accumulated during an entire operational window. These types of events could be stellar activities such as solar flares or even originated outside the solar system in the form of gamma-ray bursts and other phenomena which may immediately damage SV components.

On Earth electrical systems are largely shielded from such events and solar radiation by the atmosphere and electromagnetic fields of Earth. In space, shielding can and often is implemented to help prevent radiation from presenting an unacceptable level of risk toward mission accomplishment. This will vary depending on the type of SV and the purpose and importance of its mission. Designers of a small satellite, with a planned operational window of only one year, may decide that the weight and space taken up by such shielding would not be worth the protection from accumulated radiation. Since the SV is not intended to operate long enough for that to become an issue, it would potentially be a waste of other resources if the risk were not simply accepted. In this type of situation, the SV would presumably be rolling the dice on a singular event hitting the unshielded system and damaging it. Other systems with longer operational windows of multiple years or decades may choose to shield from radiation some or all of their components. This would specifically be the case on systems where human life is also in the balance such as commercial space flight, government space programs, and complex systems like the space station.

Temperature

Though less prone to irregular or singular events that could impact SV operations, the extremes and swings of temperature in space can have impacts on the electrical computing systems. With radiation some aspects were largely predictable such as exposure to solar radiation and how that energy would accumulate over time in onboard components. Temperature is coped with in a similar manner to radiation where the SV has to be built to certain standards to survive normal life in space but also could receive insulating coatings and materials to prolong the SV life in the face of long-term exposure to the swings and excesses of hot and cold in space.

There is also a similar tradeoff to radiation mitigation in coping with the further ends of temperature measurements a SV may be exposed to. Weight and bulkiness of SV components will tend to grow as these types of solutions are applied and may not have adequate cost benefit in extending the SV life cycle to be worth applying. Many missions will find the line of acceptable risk for temperature exposure and work to that. This is mostly considering orbital systems around the Earth where we have good, reliable, and regular data on temperature variations and can make well-informed risk acceptance decisions. This becomes much more difficult when considering SVs that will not be on a regular orbit or orbit at all and where temperature data may be less well known and more dangerous to the spacecraft.

Space Objects and Collisions

There is a lot of junk orbiting our planet. Each time humans launch a satellite or rock or put anything high enough above the Earth, we are potentially leaving it there for years, decades, or longer. Additionally, there are several specific orbital elevations and planes that are specifically suited to the operations of different kinds of SVs with different missions. As such, these locations in the space around our planet are particularly crowded. Don't get me wrong, space is big, really big, even in the immediate orbital vicinity of our planet. That doesn't mean though that collisions can't and don't happen, they do and will increase in probability as space becomes more widely accessible.

There are essentially two types of things in outer space, those we put there and those that are naturally occurring. In our near-term future operating in space, the greater danger to SVs is posed by debris and junk as well as other operating SVs residing in the space around the planet. As with the other space challenges we have covered, space objects present another opportunity for risk acceptance and/or avoidance. If a collision is likely between space objects, those operating those objects can either accept the risk or avoid it. In accepting risk, the operator has hope that the odds of the objects actually making contact in their passing near each other are low enough to not actively deal with.

Close enough for potential collision may be calculated by one SV operator as passing within a mile of another object in space. That is still a pretty wide margin, and in some situations the decision may be to maneuver the vehicle to a slightly different orbit to avoid the other object. In some situations where the SV does not have its own position or attitude adjustment capabilities, there may be no choice at all, only an ability to observe. This brings us to an interesting point. If one SV cannot maneuver and is on a potential collision course with another SV that can, does the maneuvering vehicle get to send a bill to the non-maneuvering SV for wasting part of its propulsion capabilities or mission window on maneuver? This may seem ridiculous if one cannot maneuver, but what if both can, and one operator makes a decision to accept the risk and the other to avoid it? What if the SVs are owned by different corporations or countries? There is no currently well-established legal doctrine dictating how operators of SVs should behave in such situations and where things like liability and costs should fall or be split.

Less complicated from a logical and decision-making perspective but perhaps far harder to implement is the avoidance of naturally occurring space objects. Imagine a scenario where a comet is passing close enough to the Earth that it passes through a popular orbital plan. It leaves a trail of ice and debris behind it during its pass of the Earth and now hundreds or thousands of SVs may need to attempt avoidance maneuvers. There are also natural space object considerations necessary as we look to missions that are more and more frequently going to leave the relatively well-known and friendly confines of Earth's orbit.

Gravity

The earliest challenge presented to space operations of all shapes and sizes is gravity. You have to get your SV far enough away from Earth and travelling at the right direction and speed to economically stay within the space domain and not burn up in the atmosphere or crash to Earth. The struggle of early space programs was escaping the pull of gravity to even initially achieve space flight and eventual orbit of the Earth. Now, the SVs orbiting the planet are more concerned with maintaining the right speeds and trajectories to keep falling around the Earth and not into it.

We are now at a point in modern-day space operations where it is again a tradeoff instead of a direct challenge. If a SV needs to orbit close to Earth for the purpose of its mission, where is the acceptable tradeoff with how close it orbits because it will be falling/travelling at higher speeds and will require more energy or propulsion to maintain that orbit and not fall into Earth? On the other hand, it may be acceptable to degrade the performance of the mission slightly by orbiting higher but expending fewer resources to do so and having an extended operational life span.

Like the challenge of temperatures in space, understanding of the gravitational effects around the planet is very mature, and there is a lot of flight heritage to base risk decisions on with regard to addressing gravity during the launch and operation of a SV. The same cannot be said as we move further away from the planet. It was a lot more complicated to figure out the impacts of gravity on the long-duration missions to the moon than it was to understand how gravity affected the orbits of earthbound satellites. The complexity of the gravity problem will only increase as we move further from Earth and conduct increasingly complicated extraterrestrial or interstellar missions.

Operational Challenges

Operational challenges are those introduced to space systems during the course of their development and operation within the space domain but not presented by the domain itself. Environmental challenges represented what must be understood and overcome to simply be in space; the operational challenges represent what must be accomplished to carry out missions and operational life spans of the SV portion of space systems.

Testing

There is a whole lot of testing that goes into the validation of a SV's ability to survive and operate as intended in outer space. A lot of testing is a check on whether or not the vehicle will survive the environmental challenges we previously discussed. At first it may be hard to accept that testing of the SV as a validation for space flight wouldn't make a lot of sense as a challenge for operations, but it is very much so that. Let's start with SVs are expensive, even small satellites, often known as smallsats or cubesat; the size of a loaf of bread can be multimillion-dollar programs. Components are expensive, testing is expensive, and launch is expensive.

Before you are comfortable launching your satellite into space, you want to make sure it can handle being in space and also will function after the launch itself. You have a couple options. You can build an expensive exact replica of your SV and subject it to environmental testing to see if your operationally intended unit is likely to survive. On the other hand, you can take the operationally intended SV itself, not build a copy, and subject the operational article to testing. This testing can cover many different aspects of what the SV will face in space. You will want to test it for its ability to survive temperature extremes and swings. You will want to test it in a vacuum similar to what it will operate within in outer space, you may want to test how it handles radiation exposure, and you definitely will want to test whether the vibrations it will encounter during launch will affect its deployment and operation.

To accomplish this testing, you have either spent a bunch of money, time, and resources assembling a SV article to be used solely for testing or you risk using the operational article or articles, and they could be damaged during testing to the point where you miss your assigned ride into outer space or have to scrap the program all together. Make no mistake, places that can subject SVs to such testing are also not cheap and are not prevalent so scheduling and paying for such tests are also highly impactful decisions to the overall success of a space system operation.

Launch

Whether a space system is operated by commercial entities, academic institutions, or government agencies, they all have to compete and prioritize rides for their SVs on a launch vehicle to actually get their SV(s) into space. There are multiple considerations when a space program chooses the launch vehicle it will utilize. The launch vehicle has to be available during a window that suits the planned operation of the space system. If you get a ride too soon, you may miss it due to project issues; if it is too late, your SVs' mission may no longer be relevant by the time it gets to space and becomes operational.

Beyond project management decisions surrounding launch are other issues that pose challenges to space systems. We covered how vibrations during the launch process may damage or impact the SV. Different types of rockets for different SVs subject their cargo to different levels of shaking and vibrations. Ruggedizing the SV to survive the vibrations of whatever launch vehicle is available or necessary to achieve appropriate positioning in space is an option. On the other hand, any increase to weight or form factor can increase costs of launch exponentially. It is not cheap to get a SV into space, on the order of hundreds of thousands of dollars for a loaf of bread-sized SV, with larger SVs having exponentially increased costs and lesser availability of launch vehicle choices and launch windows to utilize.

The big takeaway with regard to the challenge of launching a SV is that even if every other aspect of SV design, development, and operation were planned and implemented perfectly, launch constraints and issues could completely derail a space system before it gets started in its operational life span, and this challenge can fall completely outside the control of those in charge of the space system. Even then if everything else lines up, the launch vehicle can blow up on the launch pad or during its flight as well as potentially flying in a suboptimal trajectory which won't achieve the positioning required to place the SV into an operationally suitable orbit or flight path in outer space.

Deployment

So, your launch vehicle did its job to perfection and achieved the required position in space for the deployment of your SV. There is still present a challenge in successfully deploying from the launch vehicle and into outer space. A lot of engineering goes into how SVs are deployed from their launch vehicle, but vibrations of launch and other issues can cause deployment to not go as planned. This is another reason for the testing to be as thorough as possible.

If vibrations or temperature variations or the vacuum of space negatively impact the ability for certain latches or fasteners to unhook and let the SV leave the launch vehicle, it will never begin its operational life. If the mechanism for separation, whether mechanical or via propulsion, does not operate to an expected degree of accuracy, the vehicle may be damaged or not placed into correct or recoverable positioning. There are also portions of a SV that once separate from the launch vehicle must be themselves deployed.

This could be solar panels which need to unfold or antennas that need to unwind or extend. The same environmental and operational space challenges that affect deployment from the launch vehicle can hinder or damage these components and processes and end the space system operational window before it begins or significantly impact it. Imagine the SV had two sets of solar panels but only one deployed. Now the SV must try and conduct its operational mission with half the energy production available to it. This could take away from half of the entire operational window of the space system.

Detumble

Once the SV has successfully separated from the launch vehicle and deployed any movable components like solar panels and antennas, there is a need for stabilization. At this point, whether from the deployment or the launch vehicles' own position and rotation, the SV may be in a tumble, it may not be in exactly the right orbital plane or it may not have the necessary attitude to conduct its mission. The challenge of stabilization is present post deployment and to a certain extent is also required for position and attitude maintenance or alterations during the operation of the SV.

In some SVs and their specific missions, certain tumbles or lack of exact attitude or position may not be an issue, and stabilization need only occur to a certain extent acceptable for the operation of the SV and its mission. No matter the extent stabilization is required, it will be necessary to some degree and accomplishing stabilization involves the use of onboard resources such as electrical energy or propulsion fuel as well as time. The decision on whether to expend resources quickly to achieve stabilization or use less over a longer period to stabilize the SV falls on the operators of the SV. These decisions must be made based on the impact to the operational life span of the SV and how the expenditure of fuel or the passing of time affects the mission. In some cases, there may not be an opportunity to make such decisions; if the only option for attitude or position correction and detumbling is torque rods and momentum wheels, it may take a very long time, months even, before the SV can carry out its mission. If the operational window of the spacecraft with regard to temperature and radiation was only a year, the space system has now wasted a large percentage of its life span on stabilization. This further amplifies the need for adequate testing, well-informed decisions, and stable and expected launch and deployments.

Power

Power on a SV is an extremely constraining factor for its operation and its survival. Even after successful stabilization, and stabilization that did not require unexpected expenditures of energy or propulsion, the energy budget for a SV is deterministic in its ability to conduct its mission, stay in correct position and attitude, as well as communicate down to ground stations. We have already also discussed how unsuspected maneuvers to avoid collisions may impact the power budget of the SV. Stabilization and maneuvering may take so much of the SV's initial or stored power budget that it must spend the next orbit or two doing nothing but charging its batteries with its solar panels and not conducting mission activities or even communicating with the ground.

The operational window of a spacecraft is planned out in regard to power generation via solar panels or potentially other means, power storage via batteries, and power consumption from the bus and payload of the SV. Everything centers on the survival of the SV, which is why if the power consumption of maneuvers, stabilization, or even conducting mission activities endangers the ability of the SV to continue to fly, it must prioritize maintenance of its power budget via increased charging. The long story short of power and SVs is that there is a finite amount that can be generated and stored. Just because a SV is in orbital position to take a picture of with its payload doesn't mean that it is within the power budget to do so and maintain optimal operability. Power impacts the operational window of the SV in its totality as well as intermittently during the course of the operational life span as the SV must maintain power budget for flight even at the expense of payload operation and mission tasking.

Emanations

Wouldn't it be a shame if once the SV made it to its proper position and orbit in space, the mission conducting payload, intent on listening for certain signals, was unable to distinguish those signals from the emanations radiating from the SV itself as a result of its communications and day-to-day functions? Worse yet, emanations from a payload emitter could impact the ability of the ground station to communicate with the SV itself.

Emanation challenges are complex but can be tested for and designed around. The difficulty with emanation testing compared to some of the other testing we have discussed is that it is very difficult to replicate the quiet of space here on Earth where there are millions of radio, cell, GPS, and other signals being emitted from devices everywhere. To test whether emanations from one part of the SV will impact the functioning of other onboard components, you have to get the SV into a place where no other signals would impact the results. These types of places, known as anechoic chambers, are not very common, and testing emanations can be more expensive and hard to come by than other tests. Depending on the payload mission and bus communication methods designed for in the space system, such chambers may be required beyond nominal self-compatibility testing of emitters and sensors to address the risk of finding out in space that emanations are an insurmountable problem.

Frequency

Even beyond the emanations of the SV, there is the concept of signal pollution which may not be hugely impactful in space, but to the ground station trying to talk to the SV through all the signal noise on Earth, it can be a serious problem. Choosing the right wave frequency with which to carry out radio communications between SV and ground station is an important design decision. Frequency can impact the type of antennas, the directionality of signals possible, as well as the reliability and bandwidth available across that signal frequency.

Unfortunately, frequency is not just a challenge in regard to choosing the right type of communication signal for the SV and ground station to utilize, but it also must be available and legal. Unlike other aspects of space operations such as collision avoidance maneuvering, frequency use is an enforced aspect of space system functionality. In fact, space systems must apply and register for the frequency they would like to utilize, and it must not conflict with other frequencies of signals already in use and registered or set aside for specific emergency or military use. Similar to launch windows, this is a third-party controlled constraint where another organization is determining whether or not the frequency you say you need is OK for you to utilize. This means that frequency determination must be made early on and registration complete and successful before design and development get too far down the road. On the plus, registration of signal frequencies means there should be less impactful noise to compete with when trying to talk between the ground station and the SV. You wouldn't want to try communicating over the same frequency as cell phones as the noise level present would be extreme and may make successful communications to or from the ground station impossible.

De-orbit

Space junk and debris are a growing problem and will only exponentially increase with the accessibility of space operations. To address this, there are certain de-orbit requirements depending on where in relation to Earth your SV will operate. Whether via orbital positioning, position adjustment, or propulsion reserves, you have to be able to prove that even after the operational window of your SV has concluded, the SV will burn up in the Earth's atmosphere within a predetermined time span. This is done to declutter the popular orbital positions and planes around the planet.

Though not required of every SV, this type of requirement is something I imagine will be levied against more and more space systems moving forward to try and tamp down on the space junk problem. Thus, it must be added to the challenges of space system operation since carrying onboard propulsion for de-orbit or maintaining power creation, storage, and utilization by torque rods to enter a de-orbit trajectory far beyond the operational window of the spacecraft must be proven. This means potentially added weight, components, or other constraining attributes to an already complex operation.

Conclusion

In this chapter we covered a wide array of challenges present in the operation of space systems in general with a large focus on the challenges within the space domain faced by the SV or vehicles. Aside from understanding the challenges that cybersecurity needs to be implemented around and in support of, any security solution needs to also not increase the risk to the space system posed by any of these challenges. Additionally, it is just as important to understand the risk decisions likely to be made by the space community in regard to cybersecurity choices because they must align their risk acceptance and avoidance strategies to not only account for cybersecurity threats but those they already face in the operation of their systems.

CHAPTER 3

Low Earth Orbit

Low Earth orbit or LEO will be covered to a greater extent in this book than other types of space systems for a multitude of reasons. The most important to me is that as space becomes more reachable and feasible for varying organizations to operate within, that accessibility will begin at LEO first. Since LEO will be the most readily available portion of the space domain available to the widest potential operators, it will initially present the lion's share of computing devices in space that is in need of appropriate cybersecurity implementations.

Exact definitions of what constitutes LEO vary from organization to organization. In a general sense, a space vehicle (SV) would be considered to exist within low Earth orbit if it did not pass beyond an altitude of around 2000 kilometers or very roughly 1200 miles above the Earth. The SV also has to maintain and recur that orbit and not return to the atmosphere immediately. For those of you versed in space operations, you may have slight corrections or opinions on this, but for the basis of understanding the unique aspects of SVs within this orbit, those assumptive measurements are more than adequate.

Further, I will be concentrating on the small satellites, also known as cubesats or smallsats as I discuss LEO SVs. I will be doing this because most LEO SVs are small satellites and because cubesats have proven to be a good way of standardizing this initial and burgeoning frontier of space operations. Cubesats get their name for being one unit or one "U" which is a 10cm by 10cm by 10cm cube. Small satellites or cubesats are often referred to by their size, such as 2U, 6U, and so on. A 2U cubesat closely resembles the size of a loaf of bread. For the rest of this book, I will refer to such SVs together as smallsats.

My focus on smallsats in LEO is not to make a statement that other types of SVs in LEO are impossible or improbable to exist. On the other hand, they provide a commonly used and relatively standardized form factor present in the LEO region of space around the planet and share characteristics that impact how general space challenges apply to them as well as why they create their own specific attributes and issues.

© Jacob G. Oakley 2020
J. G. Oakley, *Cybersecurity for Space*, https://doi.org/10.1007/978-1-4842-5732-6_3

LEO, Smallsats, and the General Challenges of Space

As you would expect, having an extremely small form factor and flying at LEO present positive and negative adjustments to the general challenges of space system operations we already discussed. LEO itself and the smallsats that fly in it provide advantages and disadvantages to different mission sets that can be carried out by SVs. As will be shown with other orbits and vehicle types as well, there are also certain missions that can only be accomplished from specific orbits and that is due to their unique attributes as they apply to general space challenges and the attributes specific only to their orbit and intent.

Environmental Challenges

Due to flying closer to Earth, LEO SVs are more impacted by the Earth's atmosphere more than a more distantly orbiting or non-orbital SV would. Additionally, the atmospheric influence and proximity to the Earth change the way other environmental challenges will impact the spacecraft.

Radiation

For instance, radiation is going to have less of an impact on LEO SVs than those that venture completely beyond the protective barriers of the Earth's atmosphere and electromagnetic fields. This means that radiation absorbed throughout the life span of the SV will be less than would happen on an orbit that resided further from the planet. It also means that any singular radiation events such as solar flares will be at least somewhat muted by the time they penetrate the atmospheric and electromagnetic barriers and ultimately affect the SV.

What all this boils down to is that for LEO-orbiting SVs of any size, radiation hardening to protect from harmful bursts or accumulations is necessary to a lesser degree when considering the potential life spans of these vehicles. Risk acceptance decisions for such orbital regions are more likely to happen regarding increased radiation shielding instead of paying more for further radiation-hardened components. The byproduct of that means SVs in LEO can be of smaller form factors and weigh less since they often do not need to pack on additional radiation shielding. Of course, this is not always the case, and special payload missions or operational life spans intended to be longer than usual may still need to pursue preventative measures against radiation damage.

Temperature

Unlike radiation, temperature fluctuations are going to be more irregular for a vehicle orbiting close to Earth due to potential variations in atmospheric density. As a SV's orbit is higher above the surface of the Earth, temperature fluctuations will be more easily predicted via orbital location in the vacuum of space. As such, preparing for and making risk decisions regarding temperature for LEO devices is not necessarily a straightforward endeavor.

Space Objects

Where the general challenges of radiation and temperature are less of an issue for LEO SVs, the challenge of space objects, specifically man-made ones, is exacerbated significantly. Since LEO is the most accessible and financially feasible region of space to conduct space system operations, there are many more space objects to avoid and in a much denser area. Even though SVs in this orbital region are more likely to fall into the atmosphere and burn up, the sheer prevalence of debris, junk, and dead as well as operating SVs means it must be a regular consideration.

Since most SVs in LEO are smallsats, there are added complications due to the small form factor. Many smallsats do not have onboard propulsion and, if so, do in very small amounts. This means that the SVs in LEO are likely to have very slow maneuver capabilities like torque rods, or none at all. Due to this constraint, any maneuvers to avoid potential collisions must be orchestrated and conducted for potentially long periods of time. This may take significant portions of operational windows away from the total life span of the SV. It also means that due to the long lead time needed to actually avoid something via these mechanisms, collisions may not be predicted until it is too late to maneuver safely.

Gravity

Gravity is a two-way street for LEO SVs. On the one hand, the thrust needed to get to LEO and deploy a SV is much less than traveling further into space which means that scheduling and purchasing rides on launch vehicles are easier. Since it is an easier technological feat to enter LEO, more providers are available to get your SV there. Also, since there are more vendors and less fuel requirements, these rides are cheaper in general. Add to that the small form factor of many devices in LEO and the ride becomes even more easily attainable. A loaf of bread is a lot cheaper to get into space than a car.

On the other hand, since the SVs do not escape much of Earth's gravity by only making it into LEO, they are more impacted by it. This means that entering orbit at the right speed and trajectory is very difficult because if done incorrectly, there is relatively little time or even ability for the SV to try to correct to a more sustainable orbit. Imagine a smallsat with only torque rods and flywheels, incorrectly deployed and in an orbit that will bring it burning up in the Earth's atmosphere within 6 months. The attitude and position options available to the SV may not even have the energy to correct the SV into a longer-lasting orbit.

Even with successful deployment into the correct orbit, the effects of gravity at LEO combined with the drag from passing through the atmosphere acting on the SV mean that orbital life spans are going to be shorter in general than they would be much further from the planet's gravity. Choices to use LEO with respect to gravity center around cost and needed operational life span.

Operational Challenges

General environmental challenges to LEO SVs are mostly impacted by proximity to Earth. General operational challenges are affected by that to a degree but are also impacted by the small form factor and operational life spans available to smallsat SVs.

Testing

Testing is a pretty standardized concept for SVs of all types. Things like radiation temperature and vibration are unavoidable necessities to prevent huge wastes of time, money, and effort due to launching a SV that becomes inoperable in space. The one benefit to smallsats, which as we covered are a typical SV for LEO, is the small form factor allows for easier efforts at finding test facilities. Irregularly shaped or large SV programs may have a much more difficult time finding a facility with a vacuum chamber or oven large enough to test the SV's resilience to the elements of outer space.

Launch

I have already covered some of the benefits smallsats and SVs in LEO receive due to their form factor and the escape of gravity. One interesting thing about smallsats is they are oftentimes small enough to be deployed via the International Space Station (ISS) since they are small enough to fit in the air locks on board. Having the ability to ride-share on resupply missions to the ISS is an added perk to being small.

Deployment

In general, due to the growing standardization of single and multi-U SVs, there is less customization and fabrication needed for launch vehicles to be able to take and deploy smallsats in LEO. Additionally, smallsats are more easily deployed in groups. Some mission sets require a constellation of SVs orbiting the Earth. Having to deploy those vehicles on many separate launches can bring a level of complexity to the operation that may not be feasible, whereas being small means the same launch vehicle may be able to deploy multiple SVs of the space system at the same time and in the same orbital plane. Though certainly any dispensed members of a constellation must perform orbital maneuvering to achieve proper location within the orbital plane, doing so via a single launch is possible with the small form factor of LEO smallsats.

Stabilizing

As you may have guessed after reading the issues with space object avoidance in the "Space Objects" section, stabilizing for SVs in LEO can also be a greater challenge than faced by other sizes and locations of SVs. Small size and resources available to smallsats in LEO mean that if the SV is deployed and begins to tumble in a way that will degrade its mission, correction may be difficult or impossible. Even when not impossible, stabilization can become a very big issue when it will take a large portion of the overall intended operational life span of the SV. Also, there is the issue of being so close to Earth and not necessarily having a ton of time to course correct if the deployed trajectory of the SV will take it out of orbit.

Power

On board a SV power is the number one priority, it keeps the SV flying and the payload running. When you have small form factors, you have small batteries and small solar panels. When those are small, the SV's ability to generate and store power becomes the largest constraint on operation. Any mission conducted by a smallsat in LEO must do so on a pretty small power budget. Any issues that require power to correct, such as stabilization, mean that power could limit or prevent correction. There are other issues with power budgets being small as well; any issue with a solar panel or the deployment of that panel means the overall mission could be extremely degraded.

With power storage being limited by small batteries, it is also more likely that the SV will have to enter modes of operation where all it is doing is facing solar panels to the sun to charge. When such operations become necessary at multiple unexpected points or for long durations, the mission of the SV may be impossible to conduct with any sort of needed efficiency. Since the SV also needs power to communicate to ground stations, if the SV is constantly in power saving and charging mode, it may not be able to receive communications from the ground on how to correct to an orbit or attitude or position in space that might allow it to operate more efficiently. This means that if a component on board is also being a large power drain and needs to be updated to regulate power consumption, the power needed to communicate this to the space vehicle may be unavailable or undependable.

Unique Aspects of LEO and Smallsats

We have already covered how the orbits and form factors of LEO smallsats work to both the advantage and the disadvantage of the space system in regard to challenges of space operations. Next we will cover the specifics of LEO and smallsats that are unique in comparison to other types of SVs and orbits.

Communications

One aspect of LEO that we have yet to cover in detail is how it impacts communications windows. Since the SV is so close to Earth, it must travel at an excessively high rate of speed to continue to fall around the Earth and not into it. This means that it will orbit the Earth very quickly. This depends on the altitude within the LEO range the SV operates at, but orbiting the Earth every 90 minutes is a good example timeframe to go off of. If the SV is passing around the Earth in 90 minutes, then the time it takes to pass the horizon relative to its ground station and then be gone over the opposite horizon is a matter of minutes.

This too depends on whether the pass will happen almost directly above the ground station or closer to the horizon. It is also important to understand that many of the orbits around the Earth will not be within view of a ground station at all since the orbits progress across the face of the Earth and the SV is so close. Though the SV may circle the Earth 18 times a day, it is possible that as little as one of those is going to have a viable communication window between the ground station and the SV.

There is the added benefit that since the SV is so close to the Earth, it does not need to expend as much energy to get a communication signal to the ground. While this is helpful, the small form factor of smallsats means their antennas are smaller and the power available to send signals is also smaller. Pair that with the fact that communications windows may be over in a matter of several minutes, and there are serious constraints on how much communications are actually achievable with the SV. This is less an issue for the bus portion flying the SV but more impactful on the payload and its mission.

If we go back to the example of imagery, let's say that the SV has taken ten pictures while it was unable to communicate with our ground station. If the operators were trying a new more detailed resolution, the resulting images may actually be too big to download in a single pass over the ground station. In such a scenario hopefully, there has been engineering up front to account for the need to download chunks of files and reassemble them on the ground over the course of multiple passes.

If we can only try and get the whole picture at once otherwise it fails, then we may never be able to see the payload data. Also, at this point I will throw out consideration for hard drive management on board the SV. Hopefully protocols have been put in place for what happens when the payload hard drive fills up with images because they can't be offloaded. Among this data movement and bandwidth concern of having short communications windows also falls concerns for being able to retask the satellite, if the bus or the payload were to achieve different flight or mission requirements.

Payload and flight tasking, as well as flight and payload data download, must all be sequenced in a way that short communications windows still allow the spacecraft to function. This also does not get into cybersecurity concerns such as patching or other software changes that could potentially be necessary. Imagine having to weigh the decision to patch a critical vulnerability because it will take 20 successful passes and require the SV reboot. In Figure 3-1, the satellite on the path closer to Earth has a shorter time in the sky the ground station can see from the ground, also known as the field of view. The closer to the planet and ground station, the less time it spends in the field of view of the ground station antenna.

Figure 3-1. *Orbit Altitudes*

Ground Footprint

Where communication issues largely stem from the ground stations' ability to see the satellite at LEO, there are payload and communication issues as well with how much of the Earth the SV can see. If you have a camera payload with the mission of taking pictures of relevant spots on the Earth, the availability of those mission windows is dependent on how much of the Earth the SV can see. If it is really close, it will not have many options as far as slewing or turning the SV's camera to face the important part of the Earth because it simply won't be within the horizons the SV has.

Where communication problems were compounded by the speed of the SV and the Earth's horizon, the mission windows for, say, a camera may be just as impeded. The camera payload of a LEO smallsat may actually only be able to take pictures over targeted areas on the Earth every so many passes. The number could be every few passes or many more and must be considered as the SV is tasked and data offloaded by the ground station. With short communication and mission windows at varying times each day, a lot of planning needs to go into orchestrating a successful mission.

Using the space system requires that; tasking is created, sent to the SV, the tasking is executed, and the SV passes that mission data back down to the ground station at a later pass. If each of those activities had ten passes between them, it could mean a significant delay before an image that was tasked to the SV to be taken and make it back down to the space system operators.

Persistence

There is the concept of persistence in space operations. True persistence means the ability to always task and always execute mission and is largely unrealistic for LEO SVs. Imagining how many ground stations and satellites you would need could be extremely unrealistic. True persistence is not a viable option, but identifying what level of persistence is necessary for the success of the space system mission will drive development and design requirements for the system. Being able to task and take a picture of a specific point on Earth once a day requires far fewer SVs and ground stations than, say, doing so every 30 minutes. Another factor in persistence is the mission target. Being able to take a picture of the same point on Earth is one thing, being able to take a picture of anywhere in a certain area on the Earth becomes harder the larger the area.

Mission Persistence

The persistence of the mission is specific to, in continuance of our camera example, being able to take pictures. I have to identify how often and how large of an area I need to conduct that mission over to feed into how many SVs and on what orbits would be necessary to do so.

Communications

Communications persistence is always being able to talk to a satellite. In our current example, it does not make too much sense to have persistent communications as so far we have discussed only SVs that work on their own once tasked. In the next section, we will get into the concepts of mesh networks for SVs. Such concepts require not only some level of determined mission persistence requirement but will also require that the SVs are able to communicate in a similarly defined window to make best use of the mesh space system by tasking in a timely manner and receiving the mission data in a timely manner.

LEO Mesh Space Systems

Mesh systems are pretty self-explanatory; to achieve best case and efficient persistence, it is necessary to not only have multiple SVs and multiple ground stations within the system but to have those SVs able to communicate with each other and the ground stations able to do so as well. With enough SVs and ground stations networked together, it is much easier to be able to task any satellite from anywhere to take an image as long as one SV is over any ground station at the time of tasking. With enough SVs to close the loop around the Earth, that tasking can be communicated across the mesh to the next satellite most likely to be over the area needing a picture taken.

There are a lot of technological issues at hand in creating a mesh. How will the satellites communicate with each other? How will they route traffic across the mesh? I will not get into ways this is being addressed or attempts at doing so, but they themselves present a huge challenge for space system operation. The more satellites and ground stations, the more persistent the mission execution and tasking, but also the space system becomes more expensive and perhaps even loses the cost benefit all together of being a smallsat-comprised system operating at LEO. Those questions we will dig into in the next chapter when we discuss other types of SVs.

The Challenge of the Mesh

The real issue with the mesh is not achieving adequate persistence or getting the vehicles into space. The real challenge is understanding how the mesh will actually work and how complex payload and flight tasking could be. Let's take a relatively straightforward fictional example and say that with 50 satellites and 5 ground stations, I figure I will have a satellite over the place on Earth I need a picture taken at least every 30 minutes, and I will be able to communicate with at least 1 of those satellites every 15 minutes. That would be some pretty great persistence.

The challenge comes in when you have multiple users, with varying levels of priority all trying to task those SVs for pictures over the area of concern. How that tasking gets routed across the mesh and prioritized is itself a large problem of logic. Throw into it that, at any given moment, some of the SVs may be charging their batteries via solar panels and can't take pictures at that time. There might be a situation where a specific SV has been receiving most of the tasking due to its orbital position enabling it to take the best picture. To spread the tasking load or get a picture quicker it might become acceptable instead to take a worse angle or poorer resolution picture from one of the other SVs. How do I prioritize the shifting of tasking to slightly less optimal satellites, if they are available due to resources? These and others are all hard, operational problems that need to be addressed by any space system looking to leverage mesh type operations.

The challenge that mesh systems bring to the table that I really want to focus on is they make cybersecurity risk decisions incredibly difficult. First, you would have to figure out how to do all the other things I just covered in a satisfactory manner. Then, we would have to figure out the impact of, say, passing around a large patch across the mesh to each SV and installing and restarting each as it goes. Now around the complexities of mission tasking and flight of the mesh system, I have to know how the patch will be routed around the mesh.

I also need to know the time the SV takes as it installs and restarts around mission tasking and try to do it at points where various satellites are not around the mission area and less likely to be busy. Figuring out the amount of impact to the mesh compared to its overall operational window as a mesh is needed to appropriately make risk decisions about whether to accept the risk of cybersecurity issues or to address them via something like a patch. Figuring out the cost and benefit of doing either with regard to a mesh space system is quite a daunting task, but one that is likely to be necessary as the complexity of LEO space systems as well as others continues to evolve.

The Anomaly

Not satisfied with how difficult it is to have a successful LEO space system? Don't worry, there is one last thing SVs in low Earth orbit need to worry about. The South Atlantic Anomaly is an electromagnetic disturbance covering a large area over parts of South America and the Atlantic that will actually significantly damage and/or degrade the components and operations of SVs in LEO if they pass through it powered on. Reasons for the anomaly are not currently scientifically validated, but its presence and effects on objects that traverse its footprint and the effects they receive are. Its rough position is outlined in Figure 3-2, and any successful LEO space system must avoid having its SVs affected by it.

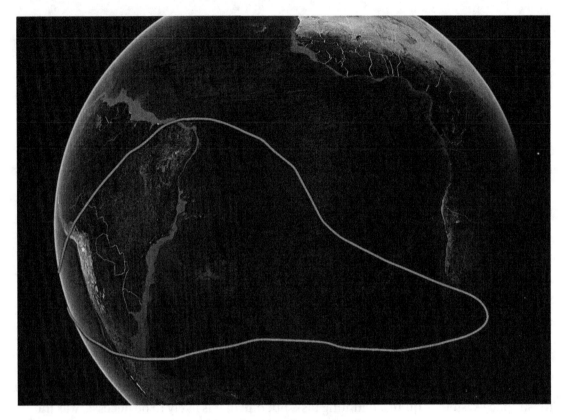

Figure 3-2. *Rough Outline of South Atlantic Anomaly*

Conclusion

In this chapter we discussed in detail the operation of smallsats in LEO. LEO and small form factors present their own advantages and disadvantages. These systems bring with them added functionality and hindered operations and must address a plethora of issues and challenges environmentally, operationally, and from the design and execution perspective. Understanding these challenges for LEO smallsats and creating ways of implementing cybersecurity around them will be a tough but necessary task as LEO is currently the most populated and easily entered area for space systems. Addressing the cybersecurity needs of LEO space systems is the most immediate problem and will translate in many ways to the continuously evolving space domain and its other types of space systems.

CHAPTER 4

Other Space Vehicles

As stated, LEO space vehicles are more representative of the immediate growth in the development and deployment of space systems. Their comparative simplicity also allows for easier analogy and framing for cyber discussions around space systems in general. There are, however, many other types of space vehicles in and beyond Earth's orbit. These systems are not limited to but include space vehicles in various orbits, complex constellations, and other special systems. I will not cover the complete catalogue of space vehicle types but go into enough detail on categorically different systems to illustrate how they all represent unique challenges and issues among the space system community and for cybersecurity implementation.

Medium Earth Orbit

Medium Earth orbit or MEO is constituted by orbits which are higher than what is considered LEO and lower than what is considered high Earth orbit or geostationary. Where LEO space vehicles may orbit the Earth in a matter of 90 minutes, MEO space vehicles essentially could have orbits as long as nearly 24 hours. Most of the space vehicles in MEO, however, orbit the Earth in between roughly 10 and 15 hours. It is in this orbit that most satellite navigation space vehicles exist, to include GPS used in Northern America as well as other foreign systems as well. Since these space vehicles are much higher above sea level and further away from the planet, they have a view of much more of the Earth than a LEO space vehicle would. Representative view areas of the three orbits are shown in Figure 4-1.

© Jacob G. Oakley 2020
J. G. Oakley, *Cybersecurity for Space*, https://doi.org/10.1007/978-1-4842-5732-6_4

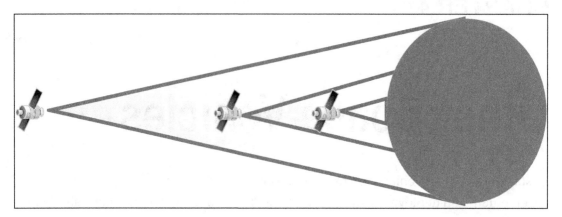

Figure 4-1. *Representative View Differences*

Since these systems are used for location based on triangulation, it is only necessary for at least three of the GPS devices to be within view of the consumer device on the ground to get a location. Since these space vehicles still progress their orbits around the planet, there is a need to have more than three for persistence over a given area, but that number is not extremely significant given the 100% persistence required to provide the triangulation and location service. Such triangulation is shown in Figure 4-2 where three GPS satellites are in view of the vehicle, allowing it to triangulate its location based on theirs.

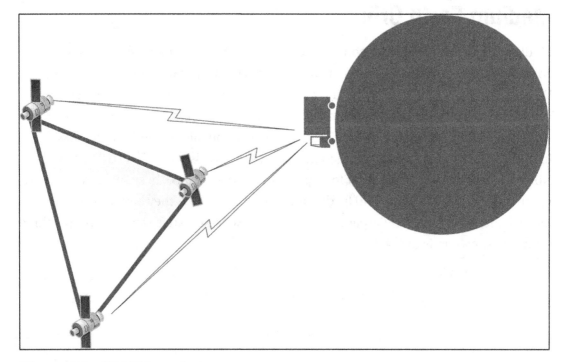

Figure 4-2. *GPS Triangulation*

Geostationary Orbit

Geostationary orbit or GEO is an orbit which has an orbital period at or longer than 24 hours. A 24-hour orbit in the same direction as the Earth's rotation, which also takes 24 hours, means the space vehicle in an equatorial orbit will always be above the same spot on Earth at all times and maintain a view of the same face of the Earth at any given time. This is ideal when it comes to monitoring activities such as the weather or looking to detect nuclear detonations over a certain portion of the Earth at all times. With GEO, one space vehicle can obtain persistence over an entire face of the Earth indefinitely as shown in Figure 4-3. The tradeoff is the size of a space vehicle necessary to accomplish such a mission and the resources required to get it in high enough an altitude for such an orbit, let alone orbital maintenance and other issues.

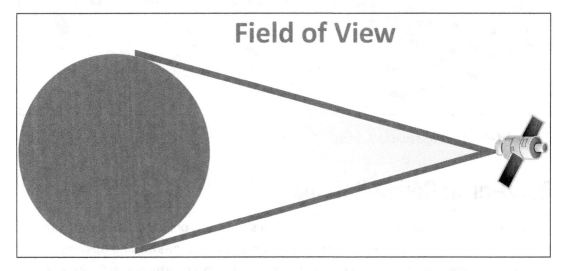

Figure 4-3. *GEO Field of View*

There are also drawbacks to having a space vehicle stationary in the sky. Say an enemy discovered it was doing a mission you did not like, in that case, jamming, otherwise impeding or avoiding detection is much easier because no orbital math is necessary to know where the satellite is or where it is looking. There are other drawbacks as well, for instance, the field of view can be large and price small for a camera capable of taking pictures of the Earth from LEO. On the other hand, a camera capable of taking useful pictures from GEO is going to be much larger and much more expensive and have a narrower field of view for imaging. The satellite itself may have a view of a whole face of the Earth, but the camera, having to focus and zoom from such distances, will quickly lose that wide field of view. Figure 4-4 shows how even though a GEO satellite may have the field of view over the whole face of the planet it sees, its ability to take focused photography of certain areas is limited to small portions of that field of view at a time.

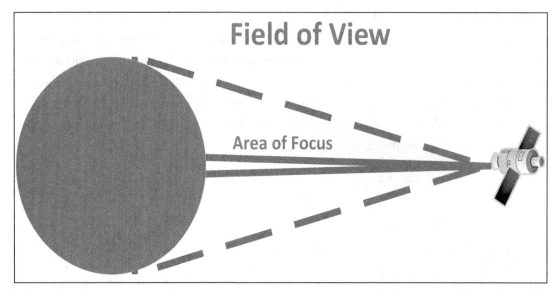

Figure 4-4. *Area of Focus vs. Field of View*

Multi-orbit Constellations

In Chapter 3, "Low Earth Orbit," we discussed mesh systems of LEO satellites and how the LEO mesh could be used to achieve greater persistence of tasking and mission over a certain area. There is also a concept of leveraging multi-orbit constellations of space vehicles in a mesh that would potentially achieve similar levels of persistence over a certain area or tasking from certain locations and with less overall space vehicles involved. At this point the cost difference in building, launching, and maintaining such a constellation will be weighed against simply using many LEO or several MEO or one MEO device to try and achieve the same effect. Using such multi-orbit constellations may make tasking persistence easier or enable greater or easier mission persistence, and the design should embrace which of these is most important, or both if necessary.

A lot would go into such a decision so we will keep the photo-imaging example and walk through how different multi-orbit constellations would impact the amount of ground that could be imaged and the quality of that image and how easily it could be tasked. If we go back to the LEO mesh example, with a certain number of ground stations and space vehicles, I can take pictures relatively often with really good quality and can task them to do so over the area of interest their orbits are geared toward relatively easy as well.

Figure 4-5 shows how LEO areas of view are much more limited and require either many ground stations near the area of interest or the LEO satellite be numerous enough to communicate with each other and fewer ground stations quickly.

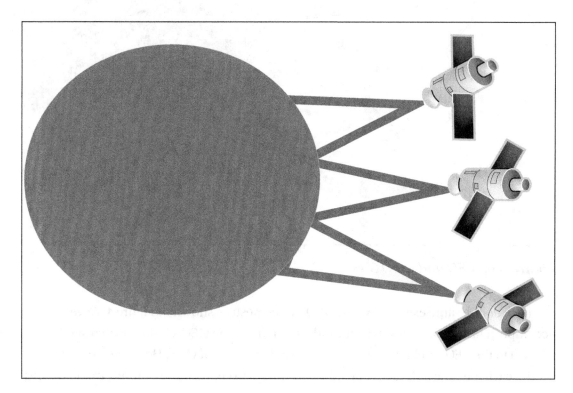

Figure 4-5. *LEO Areas of View*

Figure 4-6 shows LEO satellites using a MEO in a mesh to communicate with a ground station out of their view. Here fewer ground stations are needed because the MEO satellite is able to see large swaths of the area of interest most of the time, so as long as the ground station and the LEO vehicles are regularly in that field of view, tasking can go up to the MEO devices and then down to the LEO satellites, with collection flowing in the reverse.

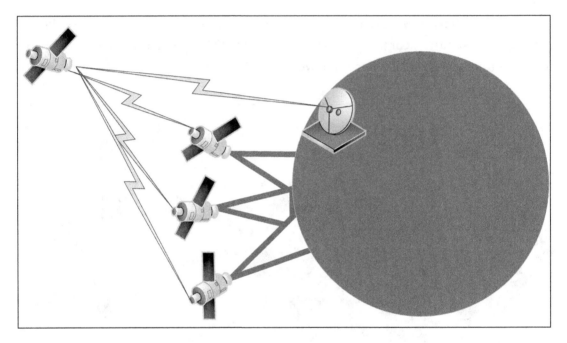

Figure 4-6. *LEO and MEO Mesh*

If we do the same exercise with a GEO in the mesh as shown in Figure 4-7, we can accomplish tasking from a single ground station up to the GEO satellite which sends it down to the LEO satellites as long as they are in its field of view. Here the greatest sacrifice will be time as it takes considerably longer to get communications traffic up and down from GEO.

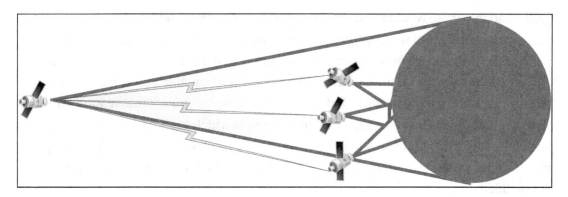

Figure 4-7. *LEO and GEO Mesh*

The biggest tradeoff to consider with these types of constellation as well as other orbits besides LEO in general is that the cost of the space vehicle being compromised likely goes up exponentially. MEO and GEO satellites are harder to build, more expensive, harder to launch, and harder to even get on a launch vehicle. Any cyber compromise of such systems will have a much higher financial impact than bringing down a LEO satellite. Further, the mission of payloads on MEO and GEO satellites has a much broader customer base. GPS or satellite radio or nuclear detection monitoring and weather satellites being tampered with or killed by an attack have a much broader impact to security and well-being than a small camera on a bread box–sized smallsat orbiting the Earth every 90 minutes.

Special Systems

Next we will cover those special space vehicles that do not orbit the Earth entirely or ones that have humans on board.

Weapons

Certain weapon systems could readily be classified as space vehicles as they themselves traverse high enough above the atmosphere and partly or wholly orbit the Earth on the way to their destination. It may seem an odd inclusion in a cybersecurity book about space systems, but weapons these days are not simple fire-and-forget munitions. Many of these weapons can be steered or altered in the course up until the moment of impact. There are also defensive systems which also operate at times in space to defeat such weapons; these would be interceptors and other systems designed to nullify the offensive capabilities of weapons that leverage space as a point from which to strike.

Whether a defensive or offensive weapon system, such space vehicles suffer from the same cybersecurity shortcomings as the more typical satellite in that if the ground station attack surface is compromised, there is little done to protect the weapon mission once it is launched. The benefit here is the window in which to try and enact an effect or for something to go wrong on a weapon is very short. However, any issue with a weapon system could mean the intended target is not struck or the intended enemy weapon is not nullified.

Human Aboard

With huge pushes from the commercial sector, the amount of space vehicles each year that carry a human on board will increase significantly. This raises many complicating factors from a security and operational standpoint compared to operating satellites. As space tourism becomes more common, we will increasingly be in a place where the cybersecurity of space vehicles is just as important to preserving onboard life as other aspects of design and test validation before space vehicles enter use.

For now, space tourism and those space vehicles of government sponsorship with humans on board are all operating in essentially a low Earth orbit. The International Space Station, for instance, and Virgin Galactic test flights for its space tourism both stayed in LEO. Regardless of whether these humans carrying space vehicles orbit like the ISS or are only in space for a short flight like a space tourism launch, the one thing in common is the human life on board that must be protected. In such space vehicles, there still exists a bus to payload relationship where part of the onboard resources fly the vehicle and others carry out the mission. The difference here from other types of vehicles is that the human lives on board are the primary mission no matter what that space vehicle is sent to do. The astronauts fixing the Hubble telescope, for instance, the mission was to fix the telescope but much higher precedent was given to the lives of the astronauts; had they been unable to conduct the repair mission due to a needed return to the shuttle or Earth, the mission of protecting human life would have still been successful.

There is also a business and industry side to this for not only commercial space flight but NASA and other international government space agencies as well. It becomes a lot harder to fund space shuttle missions or missions to the Moon and other ideas when there is a loss of human life involved. The public and the government get shy of how bad it looks when its citizens die in outer space, and as such events like challenger can set a space program very far back in a nation's priority or kill such programs all together. This is further magnified when it involves civilians instead of trained military and government astronauts. Imagine one of the first space tourism space vehicles had an issue and a loss of human life involved. Not only would the company involved likely go under, there is a risk to the entire commercial space industry if the potential customer base is too afraid to pay for the services. This is a rather cold sentiment but look at what recent crashes have done to specific airline vendors, and commercial air flight is a decade established safe way of travel. Those facts did nothing to stop countries from grounding planes from that vendor and the vendor itself and wider industry taking hits. A newly birthed commercial space industry would likely not survive such a catastrophe, even less so if the crash was caused not by physical fault but due to malicious access of a cyber system.

Extraterrestrial

These are space vehicles and systems that exist partially or wholly off of the Earth and outside its orbit. They are complex systems such as positioning satellites orbiting Mars to help systems on the surface geolocate. Systems like the rover on Mars, remote control vehicles on the Moon, as well as the landers multiple manned missions to the Moon took. These systems are susceptible to a huge swath of issues due to not being protected at all by Earth's electromagnetic field or atmosphere. At times and as extraterrestrial systems evolve and advanced, they may also make it to planets with hostile environments where space would actually have been safer for the space vehicle.

If we consider what communications windows to such space vehicles would be from a ground station on Earth, it would certainly be complicated. You would not only be competing with the orbital altitude and speed of an Earth orbiting vehicle but ones potentially orbiting bodies that are on separate orbits around the sun, for example. Adding to that complexity is the fact that when on a body like Mars, that planet has its own rotations as well. Figuring out how to operate, task, and communicate to such devices is difficult enough with complex mechanics involved in when and where we are able to communicate to, say, a space vehicle on or orbiting Mars and a ground station on Earth.

Delays for such communications would also change with the increasing and decreasing difference between planetary bodies for communications to traverse. Though no extraterrestrial locations currently house humans, it is easy to see that several nations have goals of putting, at least temporary, humans on board such space systems. Communication and power as well as other living resources will be difficult to implement, and resource-sensitive cybersecurity solutions for space will help any effort be applicable to a multitude of space vehicles as well as being tailored to each type specifically.

Deep Space

Taking the idea of communications taking exceptionally long and having rare times in view of a ground station on Earth are space vehicles operating much further out from Earth than the Moon or Mars. The best current example of this type of system is the Voyager spacecraft and other deep space missions being operated from Earth. When communications take hours long to get to and from such devices, it is currently hard to imagine implementing security from them as the average attacker or even nation state could easily communicate with a space device that is now further away than Pluto.

That is no reason not to begin assessing how security should be applied in such systems; as their resources and communications grow in complexity and effectiveness and as more than LEO becomes readily accessible, we will quickly find ourselves in a state where we do need to implement some security in such an environment. Worse is the fact that such systems take decades or longer to complete their operational mission. This means that if something were to impede or prevent the space vehicle to perform its mission or communicate, a great amount of resources will be for naught and scientific data left uncollected by Earth. This is a far in the future consideration certainly, but the principal of protecting the space vehicle from failure due to a security implementation is imperative. As such, security implementations should be resource and mission sensitive as well as tailored to the type of system and mission.

Conclusion

In this chapter we covered the types of space vehicles that are out there and in need or soon to be in need of cybersecurity professionals and built-in, bottom-up cybersecurity solutions. We covered the types of non-LEO space vehicles that orbit the Earth such as MEO and GEO satellites. We also covered special types of space vehicles with their own specialized challenges due to having humans on board, extremely complex extraterrestrial vehicles, deep space targets outside the solar system entirely, or weaponized assets. Working to integrate cybersecurity across the board in all types of these systems is a task the security industry needs to get ahead of and the space industry needs to get on board with.

CHAPTER 5

Threats to the Vehicle

Threats are those characteristics, qualities, or attributes of a space system that would allow it to be compromised. In this chapter we will focus on threats to the vehicle itself. We will later discuss threats to the mission. It is fair to say that any threat to the vehicle would certainly pose a threat to the mission being conducted by the SV. While this is true, the ways in which threats to the vehicle or the mission specifically might happen or be leveraged require different vectors and efforts. As such, I will first cover the threats to the SV itself, openly acknowledging that any threat to the vehicle likely impedes the mission as well.

These threats all have the potential to result in a no longer functioning SV. This may be due to the destruction of the SV, depriving it of resources or giving the appearance that it is no longer functioning at all to the consumers and operators on the ground. Though I will go into watchdog scripts later, I also acknowledge that such automated safety protocols and others like them potentially might save the SV from various threats to its existence. This is true in many different ways on many different SVs, but the fact that a watchdog script may save the SV from a threat does not change the fact that such threats are a general way a SV may stop functioning.

Once again, I will focus initially on threats that are applicable to smallsats in LEO. I have the same justification, that they are the more immediately prevalent space system facing cybersecurity issues and needing good solutions. Also, each of these threats easily translates into the more complex types of SVs which we have discussed, and any specific threats to other types of SVs which are not smallsats in LEO will also be discussed in this chapter. Additionally, while I explore threats to the SV as far as how they can be used to damage or disable it, there is a central system which ties many, if not all, of them together. The Command and Data Handling functions (C&DH) relay and direct communications around the SV. Suffice to say any cyber attack that affected C&DH functions would hamper or disable the SV. However, since the C&DH functions and aspects are typical of a computer in general and not specific to space, I will not present examples unique to this part of an SV.

© Jacob G. Oakley 2020
J. G. Oakley, *Cybersecurity for Space*, https://doi.org/10.1007/978-1-4842-5732-6_5

Electrical Power System (EPS)

Power, commonly known as the Electrical Power System (EPS), is the most critical requirement and therefore the biggest threat to successful operation of a SV. Without power the SV can't fly, communicate, run missions, or correct. Anything that goes wrong on a SV is potentially lethal to it and must be understood and protected against. Whether the power threat is manifested through natural or unforeseen environmental or operational issue or is the result of a malicious cyber attack, it must be mitigated in some way.

Non-cyber Threat to EPS 1

The first non-cyber threat I would like to touch on is an issue with the SV and its ability to generate power. This is typically done via solar panels that either are on various sides of a satellite or fold out from it post deployment. If a physical defect or damage were to impede the satellite from deploying its solar panels or the panels themselves were otherwise damaged, the power budget for normal operations of the SV might become exceptionally inefficient or all together impossible.

SVs in general but smallsats specifically have huge constraints when it comes to the ability to generate power. It would be hard to fold up and fit giant solar panels and have them deploy from a smallsat the size of a bread box. Therefore solar panels are not likely to produce exceptionally higher than necessary power generation, and if one out of two solar panels did not deploy or was damaged, it could mean that the mission window for the system has a lot less operational windows within it since the satellite will have to spend much more time facing the sun and charging than conducting mission actions like snapping photos.

Non-cyber Threat to EPS 2

The second non-cyber threat for power of a SV is the ability to store power once it is generated. SVs, especially smallsats, are not spending the majority of their mission life in view of the sun. This means that power generation, while important, must also be able to be stored for when the sun is not readily available. If a portion of the battery or one of several batteries becomes damaged, it will also limit the amount of operational time that the mission life span has available to it. With less energy stored, the SV cannot conduct too much mission actions when out of view of the sun for risk of draining too much of the stored power.

There is also the potential threat of a battery becoming damaged in a way that it ends up having a destructive effect on other parts of the SV. Imagine perhaps that a battery cracked under the stress from launch and the resulting chemical reactions damaged the SV so bad it never even turned on once it was deployed from the launch vehicle. It is true that some battery designs are more stable and safer than others like, say, lithium batteries. However, no matter how the battery is made, if it becomes cracked or damaged, it will at least limit the amount of energy the SV can store for when it is out of view of the sun. At worst it means that the SV may be destroyed from the inside.

Cyber Threat to EPS 1

Where the non-cyber threats to a SV's power come in the form of damage or failed operation, the cyber threat to power comes when code is changed on the satellite system that will also cause issues with the SV's ability to stay on power budget or maintain any balance of power production or storage. In this and all following cyber examples of threats, it is safe to assume that if an attacker has the ability to go after such threats to the SV, they also have the access and permissions to alter the SV's safeguards against such threats. In this case if code is being deployed to negatively influence the power production utilization and storage on the SV, then such an attacker can disable watchdog scripts and automatic power resets and so on.

The first cyber threat to power is where the payload is told to essentially attempt to communicate constantly, at maximum power until the battery is depleted. With this and any threat to a SV's power, there is always a chance that the SV eventually drifts through space long enough that its solar panels generate enough power that the SV essentially wakes back up. In this case, if the threat was persisted on the SV, any time it turned back on, it would just continue to broadcast maximum strength nonsensical signal into outer space until the battery and SV was dead again.

Cyber Threat to EPS 2

Another example of leveraging this threat would be if the payload was configured to either constantly sense or emit or run whatever mission it had to the point that it also drained the battery. In this example the SV's safeguard and safe boot options are also replaced by the attacker so that if the SV ever generates enough power to start back up, it will just keep blowing through its power with payload activity. These two attacks represent how both the bus and the payload can be attacked using code that makes them waste their power at a high rate and prevents safeguards from taking over and preserving the SV.

Communication

Communication threats to the SV may not have the potentially permanent or even destructive results as can be seen in power issues. Even so, a communication threat is essentially just as dangerous. Though the SV itself may survive, and even continue to function as normal, an inability to communicate with ground stations or other devices in a mesh means that to the users on the ground, the SV has ceased to function.

Non-cyber Threat to Communication 1

The first non-cyber communication threat is probably the most typical threat SVs face from known malicious actors in regard to communication. Jamming or electronic warfare is where the receiver is essentially sent overpowered or confusing signals that cause it to lose its ability to communicate effectively with remote devices. Power of signal is often a factor in jamming situations, and in LEO examples especially, the simple fact that resources are very constrained and power sources and storage very small means that effective jamming from the ground or other SVs is a real potential threat.

There are certainly ways around jamming threats. Jamming typically requires either a knowledge of the frequency that the signal communicates across or an ability to jam large swaths of frequencies. Therefore, any SV or communication device that can move around frequency ranges or has an ability to overpower the jamming signal can likely survive it. These solutions are not foolproof, but there are resiliency and mitigating methods to communicating in a jammed environment. This non-cyber threat to communication is nearly as old as over-air radio communication itself, and the arms race between jamming and anti-jamming technology is very mature.

Non-cyber Threat to Communication 2

The second non-cyber threat to communication that I will bring up is encryption. Though a necessary component of secure communications, the issue with encryption is that once implemented users of the encrypted communications link, in our case a SV and another SV or ground station, assume all further communications are safe. Just as in the jamming scenario, there is a constant arms race between encryption implementations and those trying to break encryption standards. What is important for all users of encryption but especially space systems to understand is that encryption must be viewed as only a speed bump to attack or compromise and not a safeguard.

As computing power increases exponentially, year-to-year encryption standards continue to fall to high-powered cryptanalysis. The added danger here to space systems is that if an encryption standard used between a SV and a ground station were to be compromised, the communications between the two are in the open air, open to anyone with a mind to get close enough to also view the now essentially clear text communications. Something else to keep in mind is that even with uncracked encryption, communications can still be subject to jamming. Though this non-cyber communication threat is not as complete a threat as the jamming threat, loss of secure communications may render a space system mission pointless or even dangerous and essentially kill the remaining mission window.

Cyber Threat to Communication 1

Staying with the encryption example, there are certainly cyber-enabled ways to pose a threat to communications with cyber. Instead of waiting for supercomputers to crack encryption standards, if a SV was compromised via a ground station terminal, an attacker would be utilizing the correct keys from the ground station and have no issue communicating with the satellite. Once the SV itself is compromised, the attacker could even delete or replace the encryption keys on the SV. Doing so would mean that the SV could no longer communicate with others in a mesh or the ground station since it would never make a successful communication handshake to establish encrypted communications. Worse if the attacker persisted access to the ground station and kept the new key from the SV, the attacker would in fact be the only one able to communicate with the SV for as long as it went unnoticed on the ground.

Impairing a SV's ability to perform encrypted communications kills the mission window in the same manner that the encryption being broken would. Even if the attacker did not alter fail-safes such as a fallback to unencrypted communications, the SV may be too sensitive to talk to over unencrypted signals. An attacker could always remove or damage fail-safe scripts and components with privileged access to the SV. Even if they did not, simply continuously altering encryption keys on the SV from the ground station even with unencrypted fallbacks means the mission window would be severely hampered or altogether impaired by communication issues. Such communication issues could also cause the SV to not receive important instruction from the ground on altering course to avoid collision or de-orbit as well.

Cyber Threat to Communication 2

The second cyber communication threat I will posit is more complicated but no less detrimental to the SV. The computerization of SVs in general and especially small satellites has meant that hardware modulators and demodulators and other antenna equipment have been replaced by software defined radios (SDRs). These software defined radios are essentially computers capable of shifting communications frequencies and communications attributes to match different incoming and outgoing communications requirements.

   The downside for the SV regarding cyber attacks is that this SDR is also another computer, networked to other parts of the SV that could be pivoted to by an attacker and infected with malicious code. Once access to an SDR is gained, the attacker could actually alter what the SDR thinks is correct frequencies and settings to communicate with the ground. Performing this attack and disabling safeguards that might reset the SV computers after so many days with failed communications would mean that to those on the ground, the SV would seemingly be unable to communicate or even be functioning.

Guidance, Navigation, and Control (GN&C)

GN&C ensures that the SV will not collide with other space objects, fall into the Earth's atmosphere, and burn up in de-orbit as well as maintain adequate position when necessary to communicate with the ground. Loss of navigation is detrimental or lethal to a SV, and threats to navigation must be seriously considered and mitigated when possible.

Non-cyber Threat to GN&C 1

When a small satellite or even larger satellites and other SVs are deployed from their launch vehicle, there is always going to be some level of detumbling. This is where the SV adjusts for any unwanted motion and inertia induced by leaving the launch vehicle. This might be minimal and hardly noticeable, or it could be severe and unrecoverable. There are even certain satellites that are designed to accept certain rates of rotation around certain axis and other tumbles so they can afford to expend less or no energy in detumble before performing their mission.

A tumble-related threat to navigation could be that a SV with little to no detumble capability was put into a fast spinning tumble through space when part of it did not separate from the launch vehicle on time. Catching part of the SV on the launch vehicle sent it into a fast spin from which it cannot recover. This could mean that solar panels are unable to deploy or that the SV is only able to communicate with the ground if it is able to do so at all. In this way an inability to detumble would mean that to the ground the SV is unable to function or be communicated with, meaning it can't be corrected. An uncorrected tumble means the SV can't guide to correct orbits and may collide or de-orbit. Worse if the tumble is severe enough to prevent solar panel deployment or prevent the SV from facing the sun for enough time, it will die a slow power death as well.

Non-cyber Threat to GN&C 2

A more straightforward non-cyber threat to navigation is simply the damage of the onboard GPS chip by radiation or physical event. Though there are other corrective capabilities some SVs have on board such as sun sensors or star tracker, loss of GPS is usually catastrophic. These other methods are of course less accurate than utilizing GPS triangulation with a chip, and even when on board the SV, such technologies may only be enough to somewhat correct the device and the mission window for the SV can still be significantly degraded.

Cyber Threat to GN&C 1

Cyber attacks which create incorrect navigation data or hamper the ability to navigate allow malicious attackers to impact other aspects of the SV like the payload or to ultimately disable it. In the first example, the satellites' ability to interpret GPS, star tracker, and sun sensor data can be altered such that it thinks it is facing the sun when it isn't and vice versa. If this type of attack was successful, the inability to navigate correctly would mean that the SV would be unable to turn its solar panels toward the sun, because it would always be turning them away from it in reality. This means that there is no power production and the SV will stop functioning eventually. Disabling safeguards during the cyber attack, as in the other examples, means that even if enough power is accumulated while the vehicle drifts through space for it to turn back on, when it does it will simply go back into its inaccurate behavior.

Cyber Threat to GN&C 2

Another example of navigation issue posing a cyber threat to a SV is loss of control of GN&C. An attacker could gain access to the SV and, upon doing so, put the SV on a direct collision course with another space object. Doing this and making the SV unable to communicate with ground stations as discussed in the Communication section would mean that the SV would literally be destroyed in a collision with another space object. Performing this type of attack in a constellation or a mesh could pose significant danger to multiple SVs as well.

De-orbit

In LEO SVs particularly, but other types as well, there is a requirement that after so long the SV will de-orbit and burn up in the atmosphere to keep down on the amount of junk floating around in popular orbital areas and planes. To accomplish this feat, SVs are either placed in an orbit that will naturally bring about the de-orbit of the SV or they have onboard propulsion or attitude and position adjustment capabilities that will de-orbit the SV in the appropriate time.

Non-cyber Threat to De-orbit

Subject to the environments of space, there is always a small possibility that something will confuse the SV to the point that it thinks it needs to trigger its de-orbit sequence. In such a scenario, the SV is sent burning up in the Earth's atmosphere at the incorrect time. There is also the potential that a SV has an issue with its ability to de-orbit. It is nontrivial to build guaranteed de-orbit ability after say a decade in space when the SV itself is expected to only conduct an operation window for several years.

Cyber Threat to De-orbit 1

There are essentially two ways in which the de-orbit threat can be manipulated via cyber attacks. The first is to simply create the same non-cyber situation we just discussed. In this type of attack, the malicious cyber actor alters configuration data on the SV to either make it think the requisite requirements have already been met to demand a de-orbit take place or change the requirements themselves so that the de-orbit triggers early based on a new configuration.

Cyber Threat to De-orbit 2

The second cyber attack involving de-orbit is to burn propulsion or potentially leverage reaction wheels and torque rods to the point that the SV is in an unrecoverable orbit that will cause it to fall into Earth's atmosphere ahead of schedule. In a SV with onboard propulsion, this can be done by burning through enough of the propulsion resources to get the SV so off course and falling toward the Earth at an inclination and rate which the remaining fuel cannot fix. In a SV where attitude and position adjustment is much slower using fly wheels and torque rods, there would likely also be a need to try and prevent correction from ground stations as this de-orbit attack process would take much longer.

Non-LEO Space Systems

Since the predominance of the examples discussed involve LEO satellites or satellites in general, I did want to cover a cyber and non-cyber example of an attack to SVs in the other types of space systems we have covered so far in this book.

Weapons

Space systems that are weapons incur significant risk to not only the loss of the SV but more importantly loss of human life on a potentially large scale when cyber and non-cyber threats to the system become a reality.

Non-cyber Threat to Weapons

Most examples of a weapon system that is also a space system with a SV in the upper reaches of the Earth's atmosphere or at higher altitudes are guided systems. Even though this is the case, there is the potential for such systems to drift off course in situations where the flight of the weapon or its accuracy cannot be guaranteed. In an observed and controlled weapon, when this happens, safety personnel are likely to destroy the weapon in flight as to avoid unintended consequences. When that is not possible, there is a chance that in the best-case scenario, the weapon never returns to the Earth to do its damage and is therefore ineffective for the actor that launched it. At worst this means another actor's space weapon system is not intercepted or the launched weapon impacts on unintended innocents. These examples relate to systems such as intercontinental ballistic missiles, interceptors or even hypersonic weapons.

Cyber Threat to Weapons

The least damaging attack on such weapon systems from the cyber domain would be if the workstations used by the safety personnel were compromised and any weapon system launched into space was told to self-destruct when not appropriate. More nefarious would be an attack that compromised targeting and launch systems for such devices, sending them at potentially innocent or unintended targets at unintended times. Both of these examples though do not involve a compromise on the SV itself and are not necessarily threats specific to the SV. As such weapons become more self-sufficient for targeting logic based on artificial intelligence (AI) algorithms and machine learning, there is a greater possibility that those onboard computing assets are compromised via a cyber attack and that the decisions that AI makes for the weapon once underway conflict with the intent of the individuals who launched it, likely in disastrous fashion.

Crewed

Crewed weapons obviously have humans on board with their livelihoods as a primary goal. That being said there are still threats specifically to the SV itself in these situations as well.

Non-cyber Threat to Crewed

The most realistic situation where a crewed SV is under threat is due to physical damage. This could be in the form of radiation events that fry important electronics that allow the crew to steer and manipulate the SV. It could also be due to actual kinetic damage from something like another space object impacting the SV and damaging thrust or control mechanisms. In these situations, the humans on board are not immediately at risk, but the SV is unable to be controlled or utilized adequately. With crewed SVs there is likely a link back to ground stations for support and potentially for someone on the Earth to fly the SV if necessary. Threats to crewed SVs are those that impede the ability of both those on the ground and those on board to control the SV. Additionally, where the ground station in other space systems has the potential for insider threats to carry out an attack both cyber and non-cyber, the crewed SV has this issue both at ground stations and on board.

Cyber Threat to Crewed

A cyber threat to a crewed SV is one that essentially results in the same impact to the SV that we just discussed from the non-cyber realm. Any malicious cyber attack that can lock both ground station based and onboard crew out of onboard computers or fool them into thinking things are fine when they aren't has the ability to pose huge threats to the SV itself. As we have seen with other types of SV cyber threats, such attacks can also cause the SV to damage itself in physical and irreparable ways. More on threats to the crew specifically in Chapter 6, "Threats to the Mission."

Extraterrestrial

Extraterrestrial systems have the added complication of being far from Earth with very long communication delays and rare communications windows. This means that those on the ground controlling such systems are likely not afforded opportunities to try and interfere with cyber and non-cyber threats alike from damaging the SV.

Non-cyber Threat to Extraterrestrial

Examples of threats to extraterrestrial SVs are based on fact and history. For example, a dust storm could cover the solar panels on an extraterrestrial rover such that it is unable to ever recharge its batteries and it dies in place. There is also the potential that an extraterrestrial rover becomes stuck in a crevice or between rocks or in sand. In any of these cases, extraterrestrial environments pose threats innumerable to SVs that end up in them. It is also easy to imagine how all of the already discussed threats to SVs could be easily lethal to a system operating on another planetary body.

Cyber Threat to Extraterrestrial

Because of the difficulty in operating extraterrestrial devices from Earth, the risk if a cyber attacker was able to gain access to an extraterrestrial SV is very high. No complex code solutions or orbital calculations are necessary to damage or kill an extraterrestrial SV. All an attacker would have to do is tell the SV to drive off a cliff or into a cave at the end of a transmission with Earth. By the time those on Earth realize the SV was doing something they hadn't planned on telling it to do, it is either unable to communicate ever again because it is in a cave out of reach of sunlight and signals or is in a hundred pieces in a ravine.

Deep Space

Similar to extraterrestrial systems, deep space systems have long communication delays and short and potentially rare communications windows. Instead of taking minutes to get communications between, say, Mars and Earth, the delay might now be hours or days. The risk that deep space systems have that extraterrestrial systems do not is a possibility for unknown trajectory or positions. A SV on Mars is going to stay on Mars at least so operators on Earth should know where to point communication antennas to find signals from SVs on that planet. If anything altered the course of a deep SV, this is not necessarily the case.

Non-cyber Threat to Deep Space

Continuing the altered course threat, imagine our deep space probe encountered a rock orbiting a planet or moon far from Earth or even a small interstellar object. If the deep SV was set adrift or off course, it would be a struggle and potential impossibility to find it again from Earth and direct communications at the new location and trajectory of that spacecraft. Obviously omnidirectional antennas on board such a SV would help this scenario, but it is a challenge specific to deep space that position and trajectory can become essentially unknown.

Cyber Threat to Deep Space

In the cyber threat to deep SVs, the SV is sent commands from a malicious attacker to send it in an unintended direction such that it might be lost from its operators on Earth. Moreover, if the attacker was able to execute malicious code on the SV itself, all it would take is a programming of a series of random maneuvers over the course of a few months to keep the deep SV from being found. In this instance even if the ground-based operators found it and attempted to plot its new course, it would be changing at random for a period that would likely cause it to be lost forever. Not to mention any of the already discussed threats, if implemented on a deep SV, would also cause unrecoverable impact to the SV.

Conclusion

We have covered many threats to SVs in this chapter. Many of them stem from the challenges we have discussed earlier in this book coming to fruition against SVs. This can clearly happen naturally or without cyber-enabled effects or be the result of malicious cyber activity on the SV or ground station. The big takeaway is that, for every challenge that has been overcome by the space community which allows space systems to function, cyber brings about a renewed threat that any of them could be reintroduced to the SV by a malicious attacker.

CHAPTER 6

Threats to the Mission

Threats to the space vehicle (SV) itself are in all cases a threat to the SV itself and likely to disrupt the mission of that SV as well. Threats to mission on the other hand have little to do with the type of SV the mission is being conducted from and are likely to be more specific to aspects of the mission itself and the onboard components of the SV utilized to carry out that mission. This means that threats to mission are as diverse and numerous as there are types of missions that can be executed aboard SVs in space. Despite a threat to the SV posing a subsequent threat to the mission of the SV, I am covering them differently because a cyber attack might target the SV on the whole or the mission specifically. An effect that goes after a mission and not the SV will be potentially tailored to surgically and perhaps surreptitiously impact the mission itself.

On the other hand, a threat to mission or even a partially realized threat to the SV may make the mission impossible to carry out or all together useless. Cyber attacks against the SV itself in an effort to deny, degrade, disrupt, destroy, or otherwise impede the SV would almost certainly be noticeable by the operators of that space system. Cyber attacks seeking to affect the mission by realizing threats which are specific to that mission may be much more surreptitious in nature and not realized by those operating the SV for long periods of time following the attack, if ever.

Cyber and Safeguards

Before we get into the specific missions and their related threats, I would like to take a quick moment to cover some of the onboard safeguards that many SVs including LEO smallsats may have on-board. I want to do so because those somewhat or very familiar with space systems, after reading Chapter 5, "Threats to the Vehicle," might argue that many of these cyber attacks aimed at such threats would be mitigated or nullified by already present and non-cyber-specific safeguards.

© Jacob G. Oakley 2020
J. G. Oakley, *Cybersecurity for Space*, https://doi.org/10.1007/978-1-4842-5732-6_6

Unfortunately, most cyber attacks aimed at realizing both threats to the vehicle and threats to the mission will likely be carried out by well-resourced well-informed attackers who will be able to use their access to the space system to not only realize such threats but prevent organic mitigations from being triggered or manifesting themselves. I will cover a few of the more predominant ones, but hopefully the trend and pattern that would be iterated following the placement of an attack effect on a SV becomes obvious.

Watchdogs

Watchdogs are scripts or code that are triggered by various situational characteristics of the spacecraft to invoke a feature that will attempt to automatically solve whatever issue it was that triggered the watchdog. One example of a trigger and solution that a watchdog might involve could be a navigation issue where the onboard GPS of the satellite is failing to work properly. Without the ability to point accurately toward a ground station or a mission target, the SV would essentially be dead in the water.

In such a scenario, we would want the satellite to behave on its own in a way which might overcome the challenge of a defective or disabled GPS chip. Therefore, if after so long without an ability to read appropriate data from a GPS chip, a SV may have watchdog code that forces it to start relying on some other form of pointing such as a star tracker or solar sensor. This way there is a chance the vehicle will be able to point back to a ground station and provide the operators of the space system with the information necessary to potentially fix or mitigate the broken GPS.

As an attacker, this means that any attack against navigation of a SV must also account for the watchdogs that may be in place to try and save the SV from such an issue. If the cyber attacker were only an insider executing commands from a ground station to disrupt the GPS, a watchdog may take over at some point and the operators of the space system may be able to regain control of the SV. On the other hand, if a cyber attacker gained some access and privilege on board the SV's computers themselves, outside of normal tasking, such watchdogs could be disabled. This could happen in a few ways. The attacker may delete the watchdog, change its trigger mechanism or threshold, or even alter the course of action taken by watchdog code.

Gold Copies

Gold copies are a copies of the operating system or settings for the SV that are stored on board and allow the return to a known good configuration in cases of catastrophic failure of installed software or other software-based issues. In this way a gold image is a way to revert the SV to a known good state in the event of an issue. SVs may revert upon issuing of a command from an operator via a ground station or at the direction of something like a watchdog script. This means that nearly any software attack against a SV could be overcome as long as the operator or a watchdog tasked the vehicle to re-install operating systems and settings off a gold copy.

This again disrupts a simple insider threat where a malicious space system operator tries to execute commands that are unhealthy to the SV. If caught by another operator or triggering a watchdog, the gold image will be re-installed and normal SV function reinstated. An attacker with an ability to execute operating system commands on board the SV, though, could use such access to overwrite a copy of the gold image with one which contained malicious code allowing for access to be regained or even kill the SV upon rolling back to a gold image.

Fallback Encryption

Fallback encryption is essentially just a gold image for encryption keys. In some cases, such keys are potentially less secure or they are just pre-programmed backup options that are used in failure recover situations based on predetermined logic. Such logic likely involves a certain number of unsuccessful communication attempts from a ground station where the satellite assumes something has happened to the current key and will then try with a fallback option. This safeguard prevents an attacker from preventing communications if they were to manipulate the key in memory on the device as upon enough failed communications attempt, the SV would rotate to a key the ground station is also prepared to fall back to.

Once again, if a malicious cyber actor has access to execute actual commands on the SV operating system, fallback encryption keys can be deleted or worse changed. If current and fallback keys are deleted, the SV simply becomes unresponsive, but at least the space system operators would know something was amiss. In a scarier scenario, an attacker could overwrite existing and fallback encryption keys with something only they knew, and now any time the SV passes over a ground station owned by the attacker, they are able to operate it as their own, to include pulling down any existing intelligence such as payload data like pictures or signal captures.

Resource Limits

Resource limits are hard-coded values in the operating system of the SV that support the ongoing operation of the space system and are also intended to prolong its longevity. Resource budgets constrain things like power usage and other executions on board the spacecraft in an effort to preserve battery life or make more effective use of limited power budgets.

An attacker with the proper access could simply alter these values, making the SV susceptible to self-inflicted damage, or write values so miniscule that the SV no longer allows itself to function. An attacker could also perform less sophisticated attacks against the SV by issuing it normal commands in a repetitive or nonintuitive manner that could consistently cause the SV to hit resource limits which might cause watchdogs to execute extremely often and hamper SV operation.

Sensing Missions

Now we will get on to the meat of the chapter where we discuss various missions of SVs and how those missions are uniquely threatened by normal happenstance of space system operations as well as purposeful malicious cyber operations. Sensing missions are those SV payload missions which receive or sense something about the area of interest.

In my book *Waging Cyber War* (Apress, 2019), I discuss at length cyber attacks and their anatomy. What is important to draw from that literature is the discussion of the two types of cyber attacks which manipulate an enemy sensor system. There are attacks that alter the human user perception and there are those that alter the sensor perception. When the human perception is altered by a cyber attack, it means that the sensor still collected or observed whatever it was supposed to in the correct fashion but that the data being sent back to the human does not accurately reflect what the sensor saw. A cyber attack against the sensor perception is one which alters the ability of the sensor to see what it is supposed to. In this instance, the human user may notice that something is going on with the sensor and be more suspicious of the data than if the sensor was operating normally but sending the user false information.

Radio Signal

One type of sensing mission on board a SV would be one that listened for radio signals and recorded certain data based on that mission. Though radio signals run the gamut of frequencies, a sensing mission could be tailored to one specifically at all times or several over a course of time thanks in no small part to the digitization of the equipment used like software defined radios.

Non-cyber Threat to Mission

A non-cyber threat to a radio signal sensing mission on board a SV is unexpected emanations from the SV itself. Without appropriate testing in something like an anechoic chamber with all of the components turned on, the operators would not know that once in space, the vehicle itself would put out such strong signal pollution that it would impact the ability of the sensing payload to accurately do its job. Emanation issues could also come when vibrations during launch shift some of the components or even slightly unseat a fastener or screw on board. This could lead to signals that would otherwise remain trapped within the SV leaking out and polluting the spectrum around the sensing payload.

Cyber Threat to Mission

Malicious cyber actors are probably the second most happy individuals regarding the digitization of things like radios as the space system operators themselves. With access gained via a cyber attack, an attacker could simply alter the filtering or frequency settings on board the SV such that the sensing mission can no longer be accomplished. The attacker could even make the SV think it still had the correct settings but still impede the software defined radio's ability to recognize signals appropriately. In this situation the SV is still operating seemingly normally, but its mission payload is unable to perform its functions. In a scarier situation, the cyber attacker could also start altering the files storing signal recordings themselves so that when they are downloaded by the space system operators, they show whatever the attacker wants.

Terrestrial Photo-Imagery

Terrestrial photo-imagery is a pretty self-explanatory type of sensing mission on board a SV. This payload is going to use cameras to take pictures of things within an area of interest on Earth. It is important to keep even things like cameras on board a SV as being a sensor and attackable in all the ways a sensor is.

Non-cyber Threat to Mission

There is a common occurrence in the operation of a photo-imagery in space for long durations at a time, especially a cheaper one. Small satellites with imaging capabilities, sometimes even something as simple as a GoPro camera, will after a time in space produce yellowing images. After longer durations of exposure to the constant radiation and light from our sun, such sensors can become almost blind, producing images that are almost unrecognizable from those that were taken when the mission began years earlier.

Cyber Threat to Mission

A cyber attack could produce almost an identical issue with imaging if the attacker intended to do so. Once interactively accessing the SV, an attacker could simply skew the color properties of images already captured and stored on the SV's hard drive, waiting to be offloaded, such that they looked to be yellowed as if by a sun-damaged camera. This is a rather meaningless attack against an imagery mission from a cyber perspective though because there are many more potential ways to impact a photo-imagery mission such as changing the way the camera thinks it is supposed to focus so it can no longer take clear pictures.

Terrestrial Thermal Imagery

Terrestrial thermal imagery is a similar mission set to photo-imagery where the mission payload is a sensor intent on capturing an image of something within an area of interest on Earth. The difference is that instead of visual imagery, it is capturing varied heat sensing from the area of interest to generate a thermal image of something or somewhere on Earth.

Non-cyber Threat to Mission

Something as sensitive as thermal imagery can actually suffer non-cyber threats from something as uncontrollable and hard to mitigate as a wildfire. Thick hot smoke and raging flames could prevent something like a thermal imager from detecting something beneath the ground or on it. Imagine a satellite trying to capture heat signatures of people in an area. Wildfires within the area of interest would not only be a threat to those people's lives but also prevent such a mission payload from being useful for the duration of the fire or fires.

Cyber Threat to Mission

In the case of thermal imaging payloads, taking them out of focus would be done in a different way but essentially introduce the same issue to the SV's payload as it did with a camera payload. Where a camera with malicious code ran by an attacker can't focus on certain areas or at all, the thermal payload can be similarly impacted. If an attacker were able to alter filters and the way the sensor perceived temperature and ultimately output it to a thermal image, all sorts of things could be manipulated. Carrying on the human detection mission of such a thermal payload, an attacker could make anything between 95 and 102 degrees Fahrenheit show up in the same thermal color on the resulting output image as what the ground typically is for a given time of day. In this way the sensor is still capturing the heat signature of humans on the ground, but the output seen by the space system operators would show empty areas of ground.

Terrestrial Monitoring

Where image-based sensing payloads are attempting to sense snapshots in time as the satellite passes over certain areas of interest on the Earth's surface, a monitoring payload is instead sensing all the time looking for a triggering event to then record the related data. As onboard computing and storage capabilities continue to evolve with time and given a persistent enough tasking and mission capability, there will eventually be space systems where terrestrial monitoring is almost a constant feed of a field of view or focused area of the Earth's surface.

Non-cyber Threat to Mission

Where such a monitoring sensor payload was running a mission to record video imagery of the Earth's surface, natural phenomena such as weather or fallout from volcanic eruptions would hinder the ability of the mission to be successful as normal photo-imagery recordings would not have the ability to view the Earth's surface below dense cloud cover or smoke. Terrestrial monitoring might also actually be for the purpose of identifying and monitoring different weather phenomena such as real-time tracking of things like hurricanes or tsunamis across the Earth's oceans.

Cyber Threat to Mission

Imagining a terrestrial-based space photo sensor for monitoring purpose like a giant security camera faced at the Earth, it is easy to understand the ways in which an attacker may attempt to disrupt this specific mission. An attacker could prevent the feed or video recordings from being sent down to ground stations and consumed by the space system users by having the camera output sent to a non-existent location on the SV operating system file table so that it is actually never written anywhere in nonvolatile memory like the hard drive. More sophisticated would be an attack where older imagery collection is written over more current collection at certain points to hide ground activity and make it look like something is or is not happening despite what is actually transpiring within the area being monitored.

Space Monitoring

Space monitoring shares similar characteristics with terrestrial monitoring in that it is more than just a single snapshot collected but rather recordings or ultimately a stream of information sensed from a target area out in space.

Non-cyber Threat to Mission

Such space monitoring systems face threats from other elements out in space that would pollute or confuse the sensor doing the recording. One example might be a satellite aimed at a binary pulsar, reading the flashes of radiation from that system as a way to tell time and frame other images and the like in outer space. Any event which overpowers the regular signal being transmitted by the pulsar has the potential to disrupt the time keeping of the sensor and thus impact that SV's mission. The same goes for a sensor potentially faced at the sun monitoring solar flares and other dangerous emissions from our nearest star to attempt to give warning and time for protective measures of terrestrial electronics and infrastructure. Stronger radiation bursts from further out in space would have the potential to impact readings around the time of the event or, as discussed earlier, even damage to sensor or SV due to high radiation exposure.

Cyber Threat to Mission

A cyber attack against such a monitoring sensor could either change triggers in the sensor that cause it to record events like solar flares or again attack the data at rest postrecording while it is stored on the SV. An attack like this might mean significant events out in space are missed or false positives become so numerous the mission cannot be run. In more warlike terms, such a cyber attack might be against a satellite used to detect jamming or other signals from other SVs orbiting the Earth. A cyber attack that impacted the sensor or data dissemination of sensed data from such SVs would mean that the space system operators might be blind to other nefarious acts such as jamming or other signal emissions out in space.

Space Imaging

Space imaging is one last type of sensing payload with specific threats. It is similar to the thermal and photo-imagery sensor payloads facing the Earth except that the threats faced are often space based and not necessarily originating from Earth.

Non-cyber Threat to Mission

The perfect example of a non-cyber threat to such a system is what happened with the Hubble Space Telescope where uncalibrated imagery equipment like a lens is misconfigured or improperly fabricated on Earth, and once it makes it into space, it becomes readily apparent that it will not be able to perform its mission. Famously, the Hubble telescope was put into orbit around the Earth with a lens that was unable to focus on the areas of interest it was intended to image, and an astronaut mission had to be launched to deploy corrective equipment to the device in an effort to preserve the mission. It was successful and to this day the Hubble telescope still images the stars as intended.

Cyber Threat to Mission

For complex missions on board space-based imaging systems like Hubble, if a malicious attacker were able to alter its ability to focus properly or identify locations properly it would be next to useless. Altering the way such a device processed target location inputs to flip bits and make it take long exposures of unintended targets or altering the way exterior light sources are filtered to get appropriate images would almost entirely impede the space imaging mission of such a payload.

Emitting Missions

Emitting payloads are those which send signals instead of collecting them in the form of radio or light waves. Something unique to emitting missions over the sensing counterpart is that it often takes more energy to send a signal than to receive it, and as such SVs with emitting missions are potentially more constrained by power budgets or have greater impact to system design to support adequate power production and storage.

Positioning

The first type of emitting payload we will discuss is one known by many which is a positioning payload. SVs that provide the North American GPS signal, European Galileo signal, Russian GLONASS, or Chinese BeiDou positioning signals are all emitter payloads which provide positioning signals to receivers which can view enough of them to provide good triangulation and location data.

Non-cyber Threat to Mission

A non-cyber threat to positioning satellites could be anything that prohibits enough of them being available and broadcasting in the field of view of a receiver to provide strong enough and numerous enough signals to enable triangulation. It requires at least three and often more points of reference (which are the satellites) to allow for a receiver to determine its relative location. Such an issue could be from one or more of the satellites being disabled by any number of the space based threats or simply that the receiver has moved too close to the edge of the positioning constellation footprint on Earth to reliably and continuously get a location determination. For instance, in Northeastern Russia, a GPS receiver may be able to at times determine a location based on triangulating off the GPS constellation which has an intended area of focus over North America. However, if it travels further away from that intended area of persistence for the GPS signals, it may less and less often get adequate signal strength or numbers to perform geolocation.

Cyber Threat to Mission

Worse than the failures discussed earlier and the threat they pose to positioning systems in space, malicious adversaries launching cyber attacks can do something far more dangerous. Where non-cyber threats typically make positioning emitters unavailable or unusable, a cyber attack could make them provide false data. Triangulation off of multiple SVs in a positioning payload constellation is what is used for a receiver to determine location. If the SVs have incorrect data on their own position, there is no way for accurate triangulation and any position information would be off. Worse yet would be an attack where incorrect data is manipulated with a purpose, say over a shipping lane, and causes many commercial and military vessels to run into each other or aground.

Jamming

Another example of an emitting payload is one we have touched on already in a jammer. A SV with this sort of payload emitter is attempting to impede the communications of another SV or even ground-based system. The reason for jamming could be to stop the detection of something or communications or to prevent certain weapon systems from being able to locate their intended target.

Non-cyber Threat to Mission

In a non-cyber sense, the greatest threat to successful jamming of another receiver by an emitting payload is that once jamming begins, the target can take steps to mitigate the jamming and potentially continue to operate as needed. Jamming can either be omnidirectional or directional. When the jamming signal is omnidirectional, it is not going to be as strong, and moving over the horizon or simply further away from the jamming source could allow a receiver to operate and be a threat to the jamming mission. When directional, the signal is stronger but still moving out of line of sight of the directional jamming will probably allow the receiver to function. Lastly, simply overpowering the jamming signal with a stronger send signal in a communications stream might allow for the jamming to be inadequate.

Cyber Threat to Mission

A cyber attack that alters onboard code to pose a threat to a jamming mission will do so in a similar fashion to the signal sensing mission payloads' threats. With a dependence on software defined radios to operate, jamming payloads are just as susceptible to having their settings altered by an attacker. Utilizing a software defined radio to send jamming signals means that a single satellite payload could be modified at any given time to jam a diverse set of signals. This same fact means that an attack could slightly alter the jamming signal such that the jamming is essentially ineffective against the target. This is also a scenario where the operators of the jamming payload are unlikely to be able to verify easily whether or not their jamming is effective and may waste long periods of mission payload life span thinking they are jamming their target when they are not.

Communication Missions

Communication payloads come in two typical forms but are largely different than what communications may be assumed to be. The satellite communicates in a potentially bidirectional fashion with ground stations during operation. In this sense it receives communications that give the SV tasking for flight operations for the bus or mission operations for the payload. In response the SV will communicate down payload data to be consumed by the customers of the space system operator once on the ground. This two-way communication relationship is not a mission itself though and more a function of the SV.

Broadcast

One of the two mission types for communication is a broadcast payload. In this mission, the SV receives tasking or a communications stream from the ground station of the space system operators, but the resulting outbound communication is either for all or some SVs within signal view or a large area of interest on the ground.

Non-cyber Threat to Mission

One example of such a payload would be satellite radio. In this mission there is a radio signal sent from an Earth ground station to the SV, and it sends the same signal down to a wide area, for example, North America, so that any satellite radio receivers within the area can receive the signal and output the music. This is very similar to how GPS satellites send their GPS positioning data signal out to entire areas of North America to allow for positioning across the continent. Threats to this type of payload are going to be any non-cyber issue that prevents the satellite from receiving the signal from the ground or sending it back out to the area of interest where customers have their receivers. This type of mission payload is different from many others as it does not require much mission processing or activity on board the SV besides what is required to provide the one-to-many medium for the satellite radio signal.

Cyber Threat to Mission

Similar to how a cyber attack against GPS satellites involved having improper data for positioning so that receivers deduced incorrect location, an attack against a broadcast communications satellite can also leverage receiver-specific actions via the cyber domain. An attacker with access to the satellite operating system could broadcast at any given interval an unsubscribe signal to all radio receivers where they think they are inactive due to their owner failing to pay. If this is achieved with enough frequency, all users of the satellite radio signal would not be able to listen to their radios, and the mission payload for those satellites would be essentially nonfunctioning as far as its consumers were concerned. Both satellite radio payloads and even satellite television payloads could also be abused by a cyber attack to spread disinformation, potentially causing panic in a country by saying cities were being nuked or otherwise destroyed or attacked.

Pipe

Where the broadcast communication payload is a one to many, a communication pipe payload is a pass-through communication mission. This is the typical mission of communications satellites where they provide a satellite hop for a line of communications between two points on Earth. This is beneficial where undersea cables are not available to interconnect distant landmasses or even as fallbacks to such communication mediums.

Non-cyber Threat to Mission

Similar to the other communication payload, any non-cyber threat that prevents the satellite from communicating with the intended ground stations it is acting as a pipe between will prevent the communication mission from being successful. Where in a broadcast mission, a receiver has to be within the area of emission from the transmitter to be useful, a pipe payload requires both ground stations it is allowing communication between to be in view at all times. This means either a high orbiting satellite with a wide field of view or a mesh of satellites that the pipes allow the signal to traverse across to be effective.

Cyber Threat to Mission

This pipe communication payload is essentially a routing device between two satellite ground station communications where it receives bidirectional signals from both to enable communication between them. An attacker with access to the satellite could certainly prevent such actions by altering any number of attributes of the SV. On the other hand, the attacker could also have the communications between the two parties also sent off to a third malicious ground station and allow for that attacking party to eavesdrop. Short of noticing this change in settings on board the satellite, it would also be extremely difficult if not impossible for the space system operators on the ground to notice that their communication pipe had a purposeful leak.

Weapon Missions

Weapon missions for systems that include a SV may seem like it is closer to science fiction than reality, but it is a fast-approaching fact that the space domain will be increasingly weaponized. There are essentially two kinds of weapon missions for space systems—those which traverse space but begin and end their mission terrestrially. The classic example here would be the intercontinental ballistic missile (ICBM), and the new age example would be hypersonic weapons. Where an ICBM launches from a point on Earth, enters the space domain, and then returns, a hypersonic weapon may orbit multiple times before returning to Earth and striking a target.

There are also weapon systems which are space resident and target terrestrial targets as well as space systems with SVs weaponized against other space systems. Historically the latter two examples, with the weapon on board, would be jammers, which are a part of the electronic warfare class of warfighting activities. It is important to note that kinetic in nature or not, weapons capable of carrying out warfighting activities which are based in space or pass through it will increasingly be the target of cyber attacks as will all systems. The fact that they spend part of all of their life cycle in space means that at least some of the time, physical intervention to prevent the results of a cyber attack against such a system may be impossible.

Non-cyber Threat to Mission

The easy example of a threat to a space system that has the mission of performing a warfighting action, thus making it a weapon, would be an interceptor which stops and destroys the weapon before it completes its mission. Almost simultaneous to the development of ICBMs was the development of weapon systems that can strike them along their course of flight between launch and target. Other types of weapons have threats of their own; as we have already discussed, jammers can become ineffective due to anti-jam technologies, and any weapon, kinetic or electronic, which is based on an orbital SV is at risk of being targeted by other space-based or terrestrial kinetic systems.

Cyber Threat to Mission

Similar to how a kinetic effect like an anti-satellite missile would end the weapon payload mission aboard a satellite, so too would any cyber attack which went after the vehicle itself and did not focus on the mission. Scarier is a weapon system payload on a satellite or other SVs where the attacker has leveraged onboard controls to alter targeting and launch and locked out other ground-based entities from preventing such actions. In this scenario, a malicious cyber attack could launch warfighting capabilities against the will of the owning nation and at another, in essence carrying out what would be perceived as an act of war and having far-reaching repercussions.

Life Support

What was once a unique mission to organizations like NASA and its foreign counterparts, human life in space is now in the hands of private corporations providing space tourism services. Where there were government liable, tested and evaluated space shuttles, and a space station, there will now also be corporately and potentially privately owned spacecraft responsible for safeguarding human life.

Non-cyber Threat to Mission

Tragic examples of death on board SVs are readily available from history and range in cause from launch issues, reentry issues, and the plethora of challenges the space environment presents. What is somewhat unique to space systems with a human life payload mission is the requirement to bring that payload back to Earth in exactly the same state as it left the planet. Some weapon payloads of space systems that return to Earth do not intend to preserve the SV upon the end of the mission. A space shuttle on the other hand or space tourism vehicle must return to the Earth as they left it, intact and with live humans aboard. These examples range from a space shuttle and all aboard destroyed during launch to a cosmonaut killed on reentry into Earth's atmosphere or the deaths of those cosmonauts who were the only to die in space when their SV decompressed.

Cyber Threat to Mission

All of the non-cyber examples were due to a failure of a physical system responsible for preventing catastrophe. The truly terrifying thing about both the digitization of space systems and the burgeoning space tourism industry is that all those computing devices responsible for keeping people alive aboard SVs and returning them safely to Earth are a potential threat for those lives as well if a cyber attack compromises one or multiple systems on a SV. Science fiction is rife with examples of spaceship computers being turned against the crew in one way or another, and we are approaching a time where that could be a possibility and should be addressed sooner or later by cybersecurity and space professionals together.

Other Mission Threats

Where all previous examples so far in this chapter have focused on how the mission payload itself can be at risk to cyber and non-cyber threats, there are also several mission agnostic threats that would impact the ability of the mission payload to be successful without necessarily impacting the operational life span of the SV.

Watchdog Abuse

We have already discussed watchdogs and their purpose in automatically helping a SV recover or respond to threats. A cyber attack which elicits watchdog responses at a rate that will prevent a payload mission from being conducted would be easy to accomplish with the right access to the SV. Continuously triggering the operating system to be re-installed on the flight computer will not prevent it from being able to at times communicate with the ground or perform some flight functionality but may prevent a mission from being able to gain information or positioning necessary to execute.

Bus/Payload Communications

The communications between the bus and payload of the SV are also a potential threat to the mission payload itself, regardless of the mission type, and also do not pose a threat to the bus and its flight computer and hardware. Any issue, cyber-induced or non-cyber in nature, that prevents communications between or through the bus from the payload would mean that even if the payload mission was executing as intended, the data from that mission may never make it down to Earth to be consumed by the space system operators or their customers. This would effectively negate the ability of the mission to be carried out for most of the missions discussed so far.

Conclusion

This chapter has covered a long list of missions run by space systems and shown that there are threats to missions that are specific to their payload hardware and software. There are non-cyber threats to missions and one or many ways a malicious cyber actor with the right access could also attack the mission capability. The key takeaway from this chapter is that essentially any mission type can be affected by cyber attacks and that for each threat posed to a SV mission, there is a way to induce similar effects via the cyber domain to these space domain systems.

CHAPTER 7

Pre-operational Vectors

Now that we have covered a wide range of threats to the space vehicle (SV) and the mission on board, we need to understand the vectors from which those threats will manifest themselves. The threats we discussed were entirely purposeful when performed from the cyber domain by a malicious actor. This was not the case for many of the non-cyber examples where some may have been purposefully carried out, but many others were bad happenstance or a result of environmental and other factors of space system operation.

Discussion on the vectors for such threats there will have a similar narrative. Cyber examples will likely involve a witting actor with malintent and some of the non-cyber examples may or may not involve accidents or purposefully malicious acts. Pre-operational vectors are the ways in which or opportunities for threats to reach the SV or other aspects of the space system prior to the SVs becoming mission operational in space. These pre-operational opportunities are the most prolific ways in which a SV can be targeted and the overall space mission affected as every follow-on category of threat vector involves the SV already being in space and unreachable via typical physical means.

This also means that we have an opportunity as operators and security professionals to protect against as well as detect malicious actions against a space system while we still have the ability to physically interact with and potentially repair the SV prior to operation. I will not for each delineate on whether the threat leveraging a discussed vector is mission payload specific or generally targets the SV. As you read them, I encourage you to use what you learned in Chapter 5, "Threats to the Vehicle," and Chapter 6, "Threats to the Mission," to make your own determination.

Design

The design phase represents the earliest pre-operational vector I will outline. This is not to say that there are no opportunities during the request for proposal or response and other contractual interactions for threats and risks to be incurred by a space program.

© Jacob G. Oakley 2020
J. G. Oakley, *Cybersecurity for Space*, https://doi.org/10.1007/978-1-4842-5732-6_7

I do feel though that the first regular opportunity to impact the SV and space system directly is during the design phase in which capabilities are being outlined, discussed, and solidified for eventual development. For this and follow-on vectors, I will present cyber and non-cyber scenarios where the traditional security triad of confidentiality, integrity, and availability is each impacted.

Confidentiality

In the design phase, loss of design specification confidentiality can mean the loss of a competitive edge or a loss of a nation's resource. As such, even at this early point in the space system life cycle, the impact of the design phase as a pre-operational vector is significant.

Non-cyber Threat to Confidentiality

The traditional specter of theft is a common risk over the confidentiality of any design but especially so in sensitive and competitive space systems. Physically breaking into and stealing design materials such as hard drives, computers, or even papers and presentations is a real threat to the confidentiality of a space system design. We do not often hear of a space company or government organization being physically broken into, unfortunately this type of design theft is typically the result of an insider threat. This might be a disgruntled employee or a foreign national working on a research program, perhaps at a university or research center, who is there with ulterior motives and intent on bringing such designs back to their home country and compromising their confidentiality.

Cyber Threat to Confidentiality

The benefit of stealing something such as a space system or SV design via the cyber domain is that it can simply be copied, there need not be overt evidence of a computer compromise break-in (if one was even necessary) and the original file is left in place. A remote malicious actor gaining interactive access can exfiltrate a copy of important design information via their access to anywhere in the world thanks to the Internet, and on some operating systems, there wouldn't even be evidence tied to the original file that it had been duplicated. Inside threats can also leverage the cyber domain; instead of having to copy papers or try and walk out of a facility with a hard drive or even thumb drive, they could just plug their phone into a computer and steal data over cell networks.

Integrity

During design is the earliest and perhaps most dangerous time to affect the integrity of a SV or the rest of the space system. A change to a design that impacts integrity and potentially endangers the SV could become an undetected part of the rest of the system life cycle and ultimately prevent it from ever being successful.

Non-cyber Threat to Integrity

Accidently or intentionally any alteration to design plans for a SV at this point impacts every sequential operation in the pre-operational vector past it. If the design is altered to result in the ordering of an incorrect part or something is changed that will make the SV fail early or completely, it poses a huge risk to the space system. Given that verifications will be made as the system is created and tested back to such designs, there is a chance that an integrity issue at the design phase will be incorporated and even validated down the line if it is not something that will be detected by test and evaluation procedures.

Cyber Threat to Integrity

The cyber domain is a far more dangerous and effective way of altering design files or documents in a way that will impact the integrity of the design. Where in the non-cyber sense there is plenty of opportunity to notice mistakes or even maliciously intended changes to design documents, cyber has the opportunity to alter the files and documents after they are created and validated. For example, let's suppose an attacker with access to the computer where 3D print designs were created for a 3D printer off of design specification documents.

The design document that the 3D print file was created off of could be accurate and as intended but once the file is sent to the printer to ingest it may not even be human readable. An attacker could alter or replace it at this stage between creation and ingestion with one that will result in parts being created that are not up to specification in some way and the creator would have no idea what was ingested by the printer was inaccurate. Unless this was identified in testing prior to launch, even a referencing of the design files would show that they were still as intended and yet the integrity of the design has been attacked.

Availability

Specific to the design phase, availability refers to the ability of design specifications to be accessible and available to the organization creating the space system. Since design resources are necessary throughout the system life cycle, to include for reference during operational troubleshooting, there is a need for availability of design resources across the duration of the pre-operational and operational phases of the space system.

Non-cyber Threat to Availability

Non-cyber impacts to design resource availability are as numerous as an imagination could come up with, but mostly the impact of that availability loss comes down to poor or improper redundancy planning. Things like off-site backups and redundancy resources can mitigate the impact of anything from a natural disaster to an arsonist destroying the facility or a facility where system design is taking place. Planning for physical impacts to facilities and personnel can help avoid loss of availability of design resources and should be in line with acceptable risk of losing such resources and probability of such threats.

The risk also changes as the system life cycle iterates through phases. During the actual design phase and following development, design resources are integral. Losing the design resources at this point means that they need to be completely recreated and once again made available before design or development can continue. Once the system is operational, the impact is lessened. Where such design resources might not be available for troubleshooting or problem solving there may be an impact to the operation of the space system. However, at this phase design resources are no longer inherently preventative to the overall success of the space system.

Cyber Threat to Availability

One thing that is important regarding multiple backups of design resources in multiple locations from a cyber attack perspective is that the more locations a design resource is in, the more potential attack surface exists for an attacker to exploit and go after the confidentiality of such resources. On the other hand, if a design resource is in many locations and as a cyber attacker, I am trying to affect its availability, I now have to impact multiple potentially diverse cyber targets simultaneously to create a non-availability effect. This effect is likely to be the simple deletion of design files and resources stored on computing platforms; as such to completely deny availability, all copies would need to be deleted, easier and less surreptitious for a remote interactive attacker than a non-hacker insider threat who may need to physically travel to each site to delete files.

Development

The development phase of the pre-operational vector is where the design resources are leveraged to begin crating the actual SV and other space systems. Physical components are ordered, created, and assembled as well as nonphysical aspects like code or configurations are written and committed.

Confidentiality Threat to Confidentiality

At this point in the space system life, loss of confidentiality is less a loss of competitive edge and more a revealing of potential vulnerabilities and attack surface. Revealing how certain parts were assembled or what code was created could lead to severe impacts to the system via attacks leveraging such information. As such, a loss of confidentiality in the design phase represents a holistic vulnerability from which specific vulnerabilities may be gleaned. Further, a compromise at this juncture allows for potential countermeasure development by the adversary against SV capabilities that may be more militarily oriented.

Non-cyber Threat to Confidentiality

More likely than maliciously intended, loss of confidentiality for a developmental system like this is simply the loss of the people that have the confidential knowledge in their minds from working on a program to develop a space system. Highly skilled and specialized engineering and other professionals involved in space systems are very much sought after and are a much smaller pool than is represented by the industry need. This means that halfway through developing a program, another organization or company can come in and offer more money, a cooler project, or better location to draw talent and institutional knowledge away from one space systems development to another.

When this institutional knowledge leaves, so too does some semblance of confidentiality. There is legal recourse and documentation to prevent such confidentiality loss when someone like an engineer leaves, such as nondisclosure and noncompete agreements. Such preventative measures rely on being legally appropriate and binding and assume the losing organization has the stomach or resources for a legal battle. Loss of knowledge via loss of team members is a probable and realistic non-cyber compromise of development phase confidentiality and requires non-security-related retention and legal efforts to combat.

Cyber Threat to Confidentiality

There is no need in cyber for relying on observations and knowledge gained through them by poaching a team member for employment. A cyber actor could compromise enough systems within an organization to essentially achieve the same level of observational persistence and inherently gain their own hacker-enabled institutional knowledge of a development effort.

Imagine a compromise of key systems used to document assembly and part ordering, what microphones on board those computers or team members' phones might be able to record, or what cameras on laptops, security systems, or phones might divulge of an organization's institutional development process. Worse than the loss of a team member, there is no obvious indicator aside from catching the cyber intrusion that there is a potential for confidentiality loss during the development phase. At least when a team member is poached, the original organization can be on the lookout for copycat or similar work and products coming out of the poaching organization and sue accordingly.

Integrity

The integrity of the development process is the ability for development to continue in the way that was intended by the design phase to meet the goals of eventual operation of the space system. Anything that compromises the integrity of the development phase will result in untrustworthy configurations, settings, or assembly which ultimately affect the ability for the development of the SV and overall system to meet the standards and rigor necessary for space operation. For instance, Failure Mode, Effects, and Criticality Analysis (FMECA), which is essentially an assessment of what could fail in the system, would be an attacker's playbook on making the SV fail.

Non-cyber Threat to Integrity

Mistakes are one of the greatest threats to the integrity of the development process. Where complacency or happenstance cause the development of the space system to not be done in accordance with plans and expectations, the integrity of that development has been compromised. As an example, imagine a human carrying out the torquing of various screws and fasteners across a SV component cranked several of them too tightly.

Because the procedural integrity of the development process, here an assembly section, was not maintained, there is a risk to the actual integrity of the physical SV during launch, deployment, and upon operation. Too much torque means the screws are tighter than expected, and during vibration testing, vibrations from launch or material warping due to temperature extremes, the vehicle could be partially or completely destroyed physically.

Cyber Threat to Integrity

We already discussed how a cyber actor with interactive access to design computers might be able to alter the files that feed into 3D printer configurations to alter the physical measurement specifications of a part. In the development phase, there is a more creation-related issue that could be created via the same attack surface. If the attacker instead had the part printed with a slightly different mixture of composite materials, it may result in a part that matches the dimensions of the required piece for the SV but that would not stand up to the stresses of test, launch, and operation.

Availability

Availability during development is a need for parts, components, and settings to be present at the required times during the development pipeline to enable proper assembly of the SV and space system devices. Unavailability of various pieces and widgets could impact the workflow of the development process and result in the SV missing preassigned launch windows or failing to be timely enough to meet the operational needs it was created for. In addition to affecting the customers and consumers of these systems and their data, availability at the development phase has a high impact on the producer and vendor and can impact their business outside just the space item impacted by giving them a bad reputation.

Non-cyber Threat to Availability

Though quickly growing, the space industry is a relatively small production and vendor base. This means that a given type of equipment may only be made by one of a few companies, and those companies may be small or backlogged with orders. The expertise needed to assemble space-capable equipment and integrate various pieces is also limited and provides another potential bottleneck to the development process.

This means that if a vendor goes out of business or has a physically damaging scenario happening at a production plant or assembly location, there may not be time left to resource the same item from another vendor, if one even exists. Exacerbating the small vendor and integrator pool is the fact that many space-ready and hardened components have extremely long lead time, in some instances over a year, and any issue toward the end of that timeline that makes a part unavailable could cripple a development process for a space system, setting it back over a year as well.

Cyber Threat to Availability

Where our non-cyber example cited physical issues impeding the producers and assemblers of space components, the cyber domain affords a much less overt option for attackers and risk to system owners. An attacker could target a small vendor with much less security than the large corporation or government organization building the SV and cause havoc to the whole operation by targeting small innocuous attack surface.

Why would a hacker bother trying to remotely compromise a large federal organization to impact a space systems development when all he or she would have to do is hack the mom and pop vendor providing a long lead time product and cancel it or reprioritize it behind several other fake orders. In fact, a scary situation presents itself where the space industry of one nation could be severely impacted by another with a large enough pocketbook who simply ordered huge amounts of long lead products from the limited subset of vendors, meaning any new or further orders would be on the magnitude of years away from delivery.

Supply Chain Interdiction

Supply chain interdiction is the process in which a portion of the supply chain that feeds the development process is purposefully impacted to damage or hinder the delivery of something. In our case it is a SV or related device such as ground station components. The space industry is ripe for the picking from a supply chain interdiction standpoint because of its limited vendor and skill base. As an attacker, I know that I have to canvass a much smaller footprint of vendors for vulnerability to ultimately impact a space systems development, and it is going to be much easier to identify what vendors are servicing which organizations simply due to the smaller sample size in comparison to other industries' vendor pools.

Confidentiality

The confidentiality of a supply chain is represented by the ability to keep secret from unauthorized individuals what is being ordered, who from, who it is going to, and the physical locations that item will traverse in its journey. The compromise of this confidentiality means that an attacker can tailor extremely accurate supply chain interdiction efforts against a particular space organization or system.

Non-cyber Threat to Confidentiality

The easy example for a non-cyber threat to supply chain confidentiality is obvious physical theft of items which portray the logistics information for various aspects of a systems supply chain. There are though easier and more legal means by which a non-cyber attack attempt can be made to compromise the confidentiality of a supply chain. There is nothing illegal or particularly special about simple observation. Monitoring and taking pictures either at a vendor sight or at a targeted space organization site could potentially be highly indicative of what types of parts are going to and from locations.

Paying off delivery and shipping personnel for information is also a possibility as is simple open source research on the Internet about what second- and third-party vendors support the larger ones. This type of resource also expands the supply chain attack surface as interdiction attempts could be made against simple parts, assembled parts, and assembled devices along the supply chain path. The vendor the organization bought a radio from may get its circuit boards from another company who sources some of the capacitors and chips and a third and fourth. Depending on the goal of the interdiction and subsequent alteration, the supply chain could be attacked at its most basic or most complex logistic locations.

Cyber Threat to Confidentiality

Logistics, shipping, and delivery systems are just as digitized as anything else these days. A cyber attack against small third- or fourth-party vendor or even just the shipping service would allow a remote cyber attacker to compromise the confidentiality of supply chain information likely without notice. Information gained through this cyber intelligence collection enabled via cyber exploitation can provide the same information necessary for interdiction as any non-cyber effort can.

Integrity

Affecting the integrity of the supply chain means that at some point along the creation or movement of a supply chain, provided item cannot be guaranteed to have not been altered in some way. Maintaining the integrity of a supply chain means having knowledge of each step along the way for each part provided to the ultimate assembly of a system. When you drill down into just how many vendors supply other vendors with parts or pieces or materials for their own devices, it can be an unruly if not impossible problem to keep contained. With space systems, anything from the integrity of a solder to the integrity of the mixture of metals that went into the alloy of the antenna can ultimately impact the space system, and the integrity of the entire supply chain process is as important to the operability and life span of the system as the assembly, development, and design of those components.

Non-cyber Threat to Integrity

Traditional supply chain interdiction is the process of physically finding an item or component along its shipping or storage path and altering it in some way, if not replacing it, before it moves along the logistics pipeline to the next stop along the way to a final assembled product. There are entire industries built around anti-tamper technology and tamper detection as well as international competitions at hacker conferences on defeating them. Breaking into a warehouse and replacing a space component–assembled circuit board with one which has a hardware implant on it to enable a remote attacker or kill power after so many hours of successful operation are a couple out of innumerous types of things that can be altered or replaced with physical access to an item along the supply chain.

Cyber Threat to Integrity

The cyber domain allows for an easier-to-achieve result with some instances of supply chain interdiction. Instead of having to break into a warehouse in the cover of night to replace a good part with an altered one, an attacker can simply alter some of the onboard programming of a previously completed part of the SV while working on another. Imagine a programmer finalizing operating system installation and configuration of a payload on a SV who also takes a few minutes to plug into and access the already installed and configured flight computer to alter behavior of the SV once it is deployed in space. This required no clever tradecraft to unseal and reseal a physical wrapping or casing. This is a clear example of why cyber testing and evaluation to ensure that what was intended codewise is what gets shot into space are needed just as much as the environmental and other types of test and evaluation a SV undergoes.

Availability

The availability of various supply chain items is a similar risk to any system as the availability of development resources. Any impact to the supply chain availability will subsequently impact the development process as well. Once again, the susceptibility of the current space industry means that an issue that holds up a supply chain could essentially derail a whole program due to lack of secondary and tertiary options for some items.

Non-cyber Threat to Availability

Non-cyber effects against the supply chain availability do not need to be sophisticated in nature at all. There is not necessarily the goal of sneakily replacing a good part with a compromised one, here the attack against the supply chain is simply to effect timely delivery or prevent delivery all together.

Instead of risking something as involved as an effort against the integrity of the supply chain, the damage to the space system life span could be the same if a certain part were to accidently or purposefully fall off the back of a delivery truck in transit. Imagine multiple copies of a long lead component for a constellation of SVs were all in the same box and that box happened to not complete the trip from vendor to customer due to being lost along the way. The whole program might altogether be scrapped if multiple launches were missed and a year or more added to the development timeline of a product.

Cyber Threat to Availability

As with confidentiality, the digitization of the production and shipping business means that a remote cyber attacker has the ability to impact the supply chain by altering destination and return addresses as a package travelled. Worse than the non-cyber example, there is a huge compromise to a space system program if its long lead, expensive, or sensitive parts were to, say, be shipped to the middle of Alaska and arrive with incorrect return addresses and tracking numbers. Scarier still what if those parts somehow ended up being shipped to a competitor organization or enemy country.

Testing and Validation

As we initially covered the challenges and obstacles to successful operation of things in space, we covered a multitude of environmental constraints that such systems face. The testing, evaluation, and validation process of space systems to ensure they survive in space is in itself a strenuous activity for components and the SV to undergo. It also provides additional attack surface and another pre-operational vector for threats to come from.

Confidentiality

Important information is measured and recorded about the capacity of the SV to undergo various stresses as well as its performance data from various tests and validations. A compromise to the confidentiality of that data could give a competitor an edge to know what to build to in order to have a better performing system under such tests. Such data might also enable an enemy to know what the capabilities of a system are or how to attack the SV based on its environmental resilience data.

Non-cyber Threat to Confidentiality

During test and evaluation, it is often a good idea to make sure that the way in which the SV and the ground are intended to communicate functions as intended. Software defined radios, modulators, demodulators, and other communication equipment may need to be tweaked and configurations altered to ensure that communications are working between the ground-based antennas and the SV antennas while they are both still physically accessible and not hundreds or thousands of miles apart.

Calibration and observational data used in this process, if stolen or collected by other parties' nearby antennas, could be used to tailor and enable electronic warfare capabilities such as jamming. There is some unavoidable risk to this as the transmissions between the SV and the ground will be across the air regardless of whether during test or operation, but specific data on the detailed configurations of communications settings on the radios would certainly give an attacker a leg up on jamming or otherwise interfering with said communication signals.

Cyber Threat to Confidentiality

What could be considered a cyber validation of some settings on a SV would be running scans of open ports and protocols on what computing devices were networked to each other on board the space system. Doing this allows for a mapping of potential communication pathways but also informs the developers of what vulnerabilities are remotely accessible to the onboard computers of a SV. A remote cyber attacker who can get access to the results of this type of validation would not only have a roadmap for eventual attack delivery and pivoting across the SV computers but would allow them to know specific versions of software on the SV which could feed into an effort to research and weaponize unknown zero-day vulnerabilities for said computers that would not be addressed by the validation results because they are yet to exist threats.

Integrity

The integrity of test and evaluation processes for space systems refers to the protection of those processes and their results. A compromise of this integrity means that the test performed against the system or component was not done in a manner that will adequately test the item or device being evaluated. There is also a possibility for the integrity of the test or evaluation results to be violated even when the test itself was conducted properly.

Non-cyber Threat to Integrity

In this sense of test and evaluation integrity in the pre-operational threat vector, there are plenty of situations that could come from any of the various test and evaluation procedures space systems undergo which would provide the creating and/or operating organization with a false sense of security and risk avoidance. As an example, let's say that a SV is being sent for emanation testing or radio frequency (RF) self-compatibility testing, to make sure that the emanations from the SV itself won't impede the ability of a signal sensing payload to do its mission in space.

To evaluate this an anechoic chamber is utilized to dampen any terrestrial-based signals that would skew results and provide an essentially quiet environment to measure only those signals leaking from the SV. If the sensing equipment in the anechoic chamber was not sensitive enough to detect all the various signals that might interfere with the sensing payload, or if the SV and payload themselves were not exercised through the full gamut of activities they may perform which would produce signal leakage, these tests could provide the operators with a false sense of security that once in space, no operations from the SV would provide incorrect results or interference to the sensing payload.

Cyber Threat to Integrity

Cyber attacks can affect any test and evaluation data that is created and stored on a computer. Whether testing emanations, temperature tolerance, or any number of other scenarios, if the device recording the data has it altered by malware placed there by an attacker, it would also provide improper data to the testers and ultimately the owners and operators of the SV. This might mean that the space system goes into launch and operation without knowing what its weaknesses are or likely failures will be.

Such malware could also be used to sending the development team chasing ghosts. Reporting emanation failures or other sensitive test failures that require many hours to track down, repair, and retest could hinder SV operations if not make it miss launch windows and cause parts to be reordered as they are assumed to be the issue causing an emanation or other reported failure. All of this is time wasted which can have huge impacts to the life span or even cause the space system to fail before it starts.

Availability

At this stage of pre-operation, a failure of availability means the test and evaluation process has essentially made the SV unavailable for launch and operation. Imagine that after years of development and design and then months of test and evaluation, something happened or was discovered that would cause a redesign or other issues which could take months or years to fix. As we have already discussed, this could essentially kill the respective space system program before it even has a chance to launch. This is a necessary evil of space systems.

Not only is design, development, and procurement expensive but so is launch and operation. Even at the expense of years of design and development, it is likely better to recognize a test and evaluation failure is unfixable before spending further money to put the systems or many copies of that system into space and to try and operate them. The customer of that system may also be unwilling to accept the risk of failures identified in test and evaluation for space operations. Imagine a communications satellite for special forces that had a high failure rate due to some physical flaw. It might be a low percentage failure in operation, but even a 5% chance of failure over hours of life in the balance operations may not be acceptable to rely upon by the ultimate customer of the communication payload.

Non-cyber Threat to Availability

Accidents happen and they can happen during test and evaluation. As we just discussed, even accurate test and evaluation done properly can ground a space program and for good reason. The threat that can come about due to testing a SV for space operations is that many accidents by test equipment operators may irreparably damage or completely destroy the SV. During temperature testing for cold and hot environments likely to be exposed to in space, the SV could be destroyed if the equipment operator didn't pay attention or safety and sanity checks fail.

Though space has extreme temperatures, the transition between hots and colds is not immediate, and equipment does not need to nor is designed to undergo near immediate temperature change. In the lab equipment that generates these temperatures to expose the SV to however such change is possible and if the operator accidently switched from hot to cold extremes nearly instantly, it could cause all sorts of hardware failures and damage across the SV.

Cyber Threat to Availability

Again, with cyber, it is the result of a malicious cyber attack that causes the equipment to be damaged during test and evaluation and not an accident. During a vibration test, the SV is shaken in a way that replicates the ride it will undergo aboard whatever launch vehicle it is intended to travel into space upon. These launch vehicles have their own unique vibration strengths and rates, and SVs are often designed to a specification with the vibrations of the intended launch vehicle in mind. This does not mean that the vibration testing equipment can only operate at such a resonance, and if a cyber attacker gained remote access and altered the way the test equipment for a vibration test were calibrated, it might mean that a SV meant to ride into space on a smoother launch option is shook apart on the test platform by being shaken to evaluate a much rougher launch vehicle ride that it was not designed or built for. This damage could make the SV unavailable for launch, and it could also send the testers and evaluators down an invalid rabbit hole looking for why the SV failed a test it should have passed.

General Interdiction

Earlier we went over the supply chain interdiction concept where components of a SV and their components themselves expose an attack surface to would-be attackers that would undertake efforts to place compromised items on board a SV. In space specifically but also in general, supply chain interdiction is a known way competitors and enemies go after systems in the hopes of damaging or compromising them in some way during the development and assembly process. Interdiction though is not limited to the supply chain and assembly processes.

A fully complete SV must make several trips and stops before it ends up orbiting. Notably these stops might include from the vendor of the SV to test facilities, back to the vendor and off to the eventual customer and/or launch provider. At any point in these journeys, the SV itself, fully assembled, is also at risk of interdiction or just damage due to accidents involving the transportation vehicle. Though not as specific as the pre-operational vector examples I just outlined, it is an important source of risk that must be addressed.

Conclusion

In this chapter we discussed many of the ways that cyber and non-cyber issues may present themselves as challenges and obstacles to successful space system operations and life spans. The pre-operational phase affords both attackers' and defenders' opportunity due to the physical presence and accessibility of the SV during this phase as opposed to when it is in space. These examples highlight that physical security and cybersecurity need to be stressed and incorporated into the SV during design and development. What this chapter has also highlighted is that security and cybersecurity are necessary and are integral to the success of the space system by being ingrained during the design, development, and testing phases by the entities performing those tasks as well.

CHAPTER 8

Communication Vectors

Once the space system is past its pre-operational phases and begins its operational life cycle, threat vectors that present risk to the system as a whole are now both in space and on the ground. In the next chapter, we will walk through scenarios involving operational specific vectors for space system threats. This chapter focuses on communications as a vector which are a constant battle between implementing appropriate security standards and practices and allowing for the operability that the intended mission and its customer required to justify developing and flying a space system in the first place.

Between Ground and Space

With the earliest of space-based systems, there has been a communications link in one form or another between the operators on the ground and the space vehicle (SV) in space. This has matured over the years and our understanding of radio frequencies and ability to build more efficient antennas have increased. In addition to communications-specific technologies like antennas and frequency modulation and demodulation, there has also been a digital evolution where the communications link between a ground station and a SV is computerized and as such allows more flexibility and functionality and presents a more dynamic and at times accessible cyber attack surface.

Confidentiality

Confidentiality of communications in general is a classical security problem where communications between two or more parties are understood to only be known to those parties. There is an assumption that no one besides the known communicating parties is listening and there is an expectation of privacy. Communications between ground stations and SVs have the same hopeful assumption that other parties can't talk to the SV and that other parties cannot receive data from the SV.

© Jacob G. Oakley 2020
J. G. Oakley, *Cybersecurity for Space*, https://doi.org/10.1007/978-1-4842-5732-6_8

Non-cyber Threat to Confidentiality

A non-cyber but technical-related risk to the confidentiality of ground-to-space communications is one that plagues communications in general. Poorly implemented encryption puts confidentiality at risk and gives the communicating parties a false sense of privacy and security within which they will operate until they are informed that the supposedly secure encryption they are operating within is actually compromised.

Encryption technologies and the technologies that break encryption are in an arms race as old as protected communications themselves. Earliest examples in use by historic military and political organizations were extremely low tech, involving only written language. There will certainly come a time where the encryption standards of today will become as trivial to break as the original wireless encryption protocol which can currently be broken using a pen, paper, and simple arithmetic. As such, encryption needs to be viewed more as a speed bump so that whether due to poor standards, implementation, or the eventual computational obsolescence of the encryption, the communicators are prepared to change course when their private communications are no longer secure.

There is added danger to ground-to-space communications with regard to encryption resilience since unlike over wire and other mediums, the communications, though encrypted, are constantly being transmitted across the air for anyone to listen to. This means the encryption exposes itself to extremely large and regular communication sessions that might allow an attacker to determine patterns and break the encryption.

Cyber Threat to Confidentiality

Where supposedly private and secure communications are at some point eventually going to lose that privacy, the cyber domain allows an attacker with sufficient access to create that moment whenever they need to. Ignoring attacks against keying and encryption we already covered in Chapter 5, "Threats to the Vehicle," and Chapter 6, "Threats to the Mission," there is a capacity to force a SV or even a ground station into a less secure or sophisticated form of communication. There are configurations where space systems employ backup forms of communication that use different frequencies, technologies, and potentially beacon and transmit in the clear. Though these backup communication vectors are often limited in their access to other functionalities on a SV, an attacker with interactive access to a space system could trick the SV into switching over to less secure fallback communications which are then exploitable from the ground or other space-based receivers and transmitters.

Integrity

For the sake of this chapter, we will outline the integrity of a communications stream as the ability for that communications stream to maintain truth in the data it sends and receives. If data can be injected or altered as it passes between two communications nodes, then the link between those nodes and potentially the nodes themselves cannot provide integrity in communications.

Non-cyber Threat to Integrity

In a non-cyber sense, this could be in a follow-on fashion to a failure of confidentiality. Once another party has compromised the confidentiality of communications stream and has the ability to listen to communications, they are also potentially able to then send unexpected or unauthorized communications back across the space system. In this way the integrity of that system communications link would be compromised. If at times the SV was unable to determine what commands were coming from legitimate operational sources and which were coming from enemy ground stations that had the ability to communicate with the SV, it would no longer have a reliable integrity regarding its tasking and ground-to-space communications.

Cyber Threat to Integrity

An attacker who leveraged the cyber domain and had access to one or more members of a satellite mesh would be able to potentially direct those satellites to receive tasking not only from the operators in the ground station but from an attacker-owned one. In this way, by setting a compromised satellite to listen for and receive tasking from a rogue access point, in this case an enemy-based ground station, the integrity of the communications and tasking across the mesh would be compromised, and commands could be permeated through the mesh via this method as well as using it to offload mesh gathered data as well. Unlike the non-cyber example which required a compromise of confidentiality for this to happen, the cyber example actually enables a widespread compromise of confidentiality.

Availability

Availability of communications is the ability to make and maintain communications streams between the ground and SVs in a space system. Without such availability, a space system cannot intuitively operate. Even in a system such as Sputnik, which simply broadcasts a radio signal, it was only considered to be functioning for as long as that signal was able to be detected and received on Earth. More complex systems are no different and in nearly all modern instances require bidirectional communications availability between the ground and flight systems as well as in many cases the payload for tasking and data offload.

Non-cyber Threat to Availability

We have covered aspects of jamming and their threat in general to space systems; the communication vector between the ground and SVs presents a well-rehearsed attack avenue against space systems. Terrestrial-based jammers have infinite power in comparison to the SV itself, and larger and purpose-built jamming SVs also in orbit above the Earth have capabilities allowing them to inhibit communications. In any scenario where jamming is successful enough at degrading or preventing communications between the ground and space, it means that tasking can't be taken, course corrections issued, or valuable intelligence and data offloaded to the ground and consumers. Jamming can affect not only the maintaining of a communications stream but also strictly target the initial handshake which establishes the communications stream to begin with.

Cyber Threat to Availability

Software defined radios allow cyber attackers to attack via communications from either the ground or the SV. Where both likely utilize SDRs to configure, send, and receive signals across their antennas, an attacker could alter the configurations of those devices to attack the communications stream and alter its ability to maintain strong lines of communication. An attack against the SDR at a ground station, or aboard the SV or both, could be done in a way that it isn't a complete shutdown of communications that would incur an immediate incident response action by the operators but could involve slow and low levels of degradation that simply made the communications stream between one or several ground and space systems spotty and therefore cause the operators to direct communications to other ground stations and impact the coverage and persistence of the SV or mesh of vehicles due to an operational avoidance of an issue-riddled ground station.

Between Space and Space

Space-to-space communications will present an increasingly impactful vector for risk and attack exposure to space systems. As the prevalence of meshed SVs is utilized to accomplish various missions, the communications across that mesh will increasingly be targeted in the same way ground-to-space communications are as well as in novel and specific ways to constellation and mesh configurations. Space-to-space communications may involve many low Earth orbit satellites communicating with each other, or even a less peer to peer but hub and spoke type architecture where lower orbit satellites all communicate up to higher orbit ones which then pass the signal around the Earth and/ or to the ground.

Confidentiality

Confidentiality in space-to-space communications is essentially identical to the ground-to-space confidentiality needs and issues and has many of the same pitfalls. The main difference being that a rogue access point to a satellite in the ground-to-space scenario involves a terrestrial ground station not owned and operated by the space system owner being leveraged to perform unauthorized communications with the SV. In a mesh or constellation scenario, the rogue access point is a compromised or outside SV maneuvered into place and set up to alter communications flows within the mesh architectures.

Non-cyber Threat to Confidentiality

A non-cyber issue that presents itself in the space-to-space communications threat vector involves architectural and protocol-based decisions. If space systems are not configured to speak in a point-to-point fashion but rather leverage broadcast capabilities to attempt to communicate to and from all points in the mesh at once, it would be ineffective and risky. Not only does that expose all mesh communications to essentially open air collection by other SVs or even ground stations but it would be exhaustive to onboard power budgets to try to send and receive communications from and to all devices all the time. This is also not considering the challenge to implementing a tasking and communication protocol across such a transmission medium. There is also the similar situation of protocol for communications where connection-oriented communications should be used instead of connectionless protocols. Tying in traditional computing protocols used for communication transportation, the SV architecture should leverage communications that are more like TCP and less like UDP to help prevent issues.

Cyber Threat to Confidentiality

We have already touched on how a cyber attacker could either replace encryption keys with their own or remove the encryption piece all together from communications to the ground which would allow for unauthorized transmission or even control of the SV from another ground station. This has the benefit to the operator of being a relatively noticeable issue since the appropriate ground station will likely realize that it cannot communicate with the space system or see it performing other communications or receiving other tasking. If this sort of attack was carried out on a SV-to-SV link or to enable communications from an outside the mesh or constellation it would allow for a similar compromise of the space system but in a less noticeable fashion.

Integrity

Once again, space-to-space integrity issues mimic those of the ground, with the difference being the unauthorized actions or alterations to what is being transmitted can come from a compromised SV and not necessarily a ground station.

Non-cyber Threat to Integrity

Following the example earlier, a non-cyber threat to communications integrity could involve a rogue SV belonging to another organization or country being maneuvered into position to communicate with the constellation or mesh, and due to a compromise of confidentiality in some way, that SV is able to alter information being passed across the space system, inject improper data, or otherwise damage the integrity of the mesh or constellation network. It is important as mesh and constellation use ramp-up that they consider lessons learned from terrestrial wireless networks to include 802.11 normal home and corporate wireless systems. Rogue access points and devices in those networks represent the same types of threats space systems will face. SV meshes should ensure that they maintain control and audit of the SVs communicating across the peer-to-peer network so that even if compromised the space system operator will at least be notified that there is a new and unauthorized SV present within their network.

Cyber Threat to Integrity

The non-cyber example earlier required an enemy-provided SV be integrated into a mesh and used as a rogue access point to that mesh which allowed the attacker to compromise the mesh network integrity. With cyber compromises and the cyber domain and attack surface it affords enemies and adversaries, a hacker could gain enough control of a particular SV within a mesh that it acts as an insider threat to the mesh network in the same fashion the externally introduced SV did. Again, tying in to known and already being addressed terrestrial issues, this is a problem to normal wireless networks. Not only does a peer-to-peer or access point–based wireless network need to address rogue access points and unauthorized users, it needs to be able to detect when a user on the wireless network is acting improperly or otherwise compromised.

Availability

Communications availability within the mesh is actually less impactful to the overall space system than a loss of availability from the ground to space. Even in a scenario where communications between SVs became completely unavailable, if those SVs could still communicate with ground stations, they could essentially pass required information to each other via networked ground stations if necessary. It may also be that a mesh or constellation of satellites can perform its mission just in a limited nature given only space-to-ground communications if point-to-point communications in space were to fail.

Non-cyber Threat to Availability

Space-to-ground communications require varying amounts of precision communications beams from the SV down to the ground station due to power constraints on the SV. Ground-to-space communication is not as hindered as more power can be used to get the signal into a wider area of space, and therefore less precision is necessary. In space-to-space communications which must be point to point in nature, precision is extremely necessary. When both parties in a point-to-point space communication are power constrained, it means they both must have pretty precise location information for each other in order to send the communications beams to each other across space.

This becomes an increasingly important issue when point-to-point communications utilize optical waves instead of radio waves. Optical waves can allow SVs to communicate with each other at much higher data speeds and can do so without worry of degraded performance thanks to the vacuum of space. The downside to this is that the margin for error is much smaller than radio wave communications, and precision is more of a requirement. Any non-cyber issue that impacts a SV's ability to have a precision determination of its own and other SV's locations would impact point-to-point communications' effectiveness. It also may mean that with only one point-to-point antennas, transceiver and receiver, a SV may be only able to communicate with one other at any given time.

This also means that before it can communicate with a different SV in the peer-to-peer network, it may have to maneuver so that its optical or precision radio communications capability faces that of the new SV. In a large mesh of satellites, this may introduce a problem for appropriate tasking regarding which vehicles will slew to communicate with others, which won't and when to enable efficient communications across the mesh to fully leverage it.

Cyber Threat to Availability

As you may be picking up by now, the peer-to-peer mesh concept introduces a lot of classical computer network problems to space operations. An attack on the availability of space-to-space communications that could take advantage of an age-old computer network attack would be to introduce routing loops into peer-to-peer mesh communications. In a true peer-to-peer mesh, each device or in this case SV must act as a router of traffic, passing along and processing data when necessary. An attacker with access to a SV could gain an understanding of the way data is transmitted and traffic routed across a mesh of SVs and start introducing traffic that will solicit other SVs to continuously pass information along in loops until it dies or is discarded due to time to live exceptions.

In this way traffic could be altered to flow around the mesh until it was discarded and never transmitted down to ground stations as needed. This would make the mesh unavailable for reliable communications. As SV meshes become larger and more complex in their operation, standards for how traffic is routed and passed across those meshes need to work off lessons learned from early networks and prevent this sort of attack and others from preying on such peer-to-peer networks. To this end, extremely large and complex meshes may benefit from having a small number of SVs within the mesh whose sole purpose is health and security operations for the mesh. This would allow for routing rules and other security applications to be wrapped around mesh communications and improve reliability and security of those communications.

Between Bus and Payload

The last communication vector we will highlight is one that I feel is less understood, less protected, and a potential Achilles heel for certain space systems via their SV configuration and design. In many satellites, there is a different party that flies and operates the flight components or bus of the SV that operates the payload. This means that one organization's ground station might track the SV and make sure it avoids other space objects and stays in orbit, and another organization's ground station may interact with the payload.

The consideration here is that a compromise of one or the other may eventually mean that a cyber attack executed on board the SV bus or flight systems could allow that attacker to pivot from one to the other and eventually back to the ground station and networks of an entirely different organization. Where such an example represents a need to at least logically separate the bus and payload, there are also instances where a payload may collect and offload extremely sensitive or classified information and yet the bus and flight computers are operated at an unclassified level.

Encryption could be used on board the payload to offload this data via unclassified means or project the payload from an attack on the bus, but I do not feel this issue is adequately addressed by security professionals or the space industry and could lead to the compromise of sensitive payloads via less protected flight bus systems and ground station organizations. There is also the little known or understood concept we just covered where compromise of one organization ground-based networks could actually use payload to bus links to pivot to and compromise a completely unconnected and geographically diverse ground network via the SV.

Confidentiality

In this sense confidentiality refers to the ability, when necessary, to prevent an adversary or operator of the payload or the bus from being able to read unauthorized data from the other. In some cases this is important to national security to protect the confidentiality of classified or sensitive payload data from less cleared operators of the flight bus, and in some instances it may not be worth the cost benefit if both organizations, though different, may have the same security posture.

Non-cyber Threat to Confidentiality

One of the payload types mentioned in other chapters was the communication payload where the satellite is there to provide communication pipes to different locations on the ground. An insider threat could alter the onboard configurations of such a payload to duplicate the communications going across a requested pipe and send them off to a third ground station unbeknownst to the communicants. In this example, the parties using the payload as a communication pipe between each other have no idea that the confidentiality of the communication pipe is being violated as their communications are also being sent off to a third party. This situation is similar to an attacker or admin mirroring a communications port on a switch or router to send a copy of all communications across it to a separate location. This has purpose for both security professionals and attackers.

Cyber Threat to Confidentiality

Continuing with communication payload examples, a broadcast communication payload like the ones that provide satellite radio to various customer areas around the world could be attacked via the cyber domain and altered to remove expected confidentiality as well. An attacker with access to the ground station and/or satellite providing space-based radio signals could start broadcasting to all radio receivers that they were actually subscribed, regardless if they were or not, and thus allow anyone with a satellite radio receiver to listen to the stations without a subscription. In this instance confidentiality is not so much a privacy concern but a business one where the satellite radio provider wants to keep the satellite radio services confidential only to paying customers, and an attacker could enable anyone with a receiver to listen to their services.

Integrity

Integrity across the bus and payload communication relationship refers to the ability of the payload to rely on the bus for accurate information and pass back to the ground unaltered payload data in configurations where the payload collects data and encrypts it before sending it to the bus to offload to a ground station instead of having a payload-specific communications capability with the ground.

Non-cyber Threat to Integrity

A good non-cyber example for integrity and/or reliability issues between the bus and the payload would be something that should be tested and evaluated for, but which does not always get caught. Emanations from a bus might impede a payload's ability to separately communicate with the other ground stations it talks to and vice versa. Where operators flying the SV and operators tasking the bus have separate onboard communications capabilities and ground stations, a failure to deconflict communications efforts as well as protect emanations from each other's operations impacting the other is necessary.

Cyber Threat to Integrity

Though a bus and payload may be logically and operationally separate in a digital sense, if they leverage some of the same onboard resources, there is opportunity for an attacker to go after that shared resource and impact the bus from the payload and vice versa. A payload may leverage an onboard GPS chip for triggering collection events related to its mission, and if that GPS chip is a resource shared with the flight computer and systems on board, a cyber attacker with interactive access to a bus and flight computer may be able to exploit the GPS chip in such a way that it starts reporting incorrect data which would ultimately affect the integrity of mission data produced by the payload as it was being triggered to conduct its mission over the wrong locations. This could mean taking pictures of incorrect locations or emitting jamming signals into empty space or at other unintended SVs.

Availability

Availability of bus and payload communications is important to the operation of any SVs. Security implementations that are aimed at preventing attacks from traversing this communications path must take into account potentially failing open in an effort to not provide another point of failure and risk to the space system. Further, many SVs rely on bus-to-payload communications because though they may be operated by different organizations, the payload may utilize the same antennas and SDR to communicate with the ground as the bus. Anything that denied this availability could end the space mission by preventing the payload from communicating its tasked actions and resulting data to the ground-based operators and consumers.

Non-cyber Threat to Availability

Non-cyber threats to this bus and payload communications link are essentially any issue that might occur to a shared resource. Where such an issue may not ultimately cause the SV to die on orbit, it might cause the communications between bus and payload to no longer be operational. Also any failure that forces a SV into a power conservation mode could shut down the payload operations all together to preserve power budget and turn off a payload entirely or at least prevent its data from being offloaded, not because of damage to the communication line but from forced stoppage of data offload and payload communications in an effort to preserve the SV.

Cyber Threat to Availability

Even in situations where the communications link between the bus and payload is not eliminated and compromise is not possible by a hacker from the bus to the payload systems, encrypted payload data can still be at availability risk. In configurations where a payload is passing encrypted sensitive data off to the bus for the bus to then transmit to the ground, a compromised flight computer or data handler on board the SV could be leveraged to alter the payload files in some way so that when they are received on the ground station, they are unusable. Though not outright preventing communications between the payload and the bus, this would make the communications altogether useless. Even something as simple as executing compression on the encrypted files with password protection and a password not known to the operators of the space system could make payload data sent to the ground unusable and unrecoverable.

Conclusion

The communication vector is itself a complex mechanism with various problem sets that affect space systems. Some are classic encryption and communication challenges that the space industry and security industry both historically understand. Others are emerging threats to space system communications that are well understood in the computer and network security industry but new to space. Ensuring the space industry takes lessons learned from terrestrial-based peer-to-peer networks and routing problems and implements modern security solutions to them in space is integral to protecting such systems. The security industry needs to take known solutions for these types of problems and explore tailoring them around the constraints of space operations to better provide security to space.

CHAPTER 9

Operational Vectors

Now we will address the breadth of attack surface represented by the operational vector. This is the ground station back infrastructure, networks, users, consumers, and computing equipment responsible for the complete execution of the space system mission from tasking to receiving the data from the space vehicle (SV) and ultimately getting it in the hands of the space system customers which justify its existence. Obviously, this discussion on operational vectors is more tailored in its totality to something like a satellite that has an obvious tasking, receiving, analysis, and dissemination to customer chain. That is not to say that other systems, even some of the most unique ones like space shuttles and similar future systems, won't experience many of the same issues that can come about from the operational back end of space systems.

Flight and Operation

Flight and operation refer to the ground side elements responsible for flying the SV through space safely as well as those individuals that interact with, task, and receive data from the payload or payloads on board. As Chapter 8, "Communication Vectors," laid out, in some instance these will be different organizations completely physically and logically dislocated from one another and in other instances in fact be the same organization, ground station, and people. That being said, even if SV command and control and payload operations are separated, it would be the former usually interacting with the satellite. The ground station likely makes payload data available to the payload operators. The C&DH system on the SV would likely route tasking to the payload as necessary. To completely separate these operations, there would essentially need to be two different sets of terrestrially facing antenna and communication equipment—one for those flying the SV and another for those operating the payload.

© Jacob G. Oakley 2020
J. G. Oakley, *Cybersecurity for Space*, https://doi.org/10.1007/978-1-4842-5732-6_9

Confidentiality

In many instances and due to the nature of transmitting over open air to a satellite that is difficult to hide from proper observational equipment in the sky, much of space system flight and payload operations on the SV have little confidentiality. That being said, there are efforts to obscure the intent, purpose, and sometimes location of SVs being communicated with from the ground. This might be an effort to obscure information about SV flight itself or potential payload tasking and execution. A loss of confidentiality in this sense may incur risk to the SV itself or delay information about its mission that could aid adversaries in avoiding payload execution missions. This is more of a threat to those SVs in lower altitude orbits and with less of an ability to maneuver since they are more easily tracked from Earth.

Non-cyber Threat to Confidentiality

Many times, the ground station dishes are covered by radomes. This is a ball-like structure that encapsulates the antenna and allows it to pivot and rotate within the structure without impedance. In most cases this is done to protect the antennas and prolong its operational life in climates with more severe impact. The added benefit is that from the naked eye and optical observation, the direction the antennas points and the way it slews to keep lock on spacecraft as they pass overhead is also obscured.

This keeps the potential SVs the ground station communicates with much more difficult to determine without other information and can keep certain portions and aspects of the space missions being conducted out of that ground station confidential. A compromise of this confidentiality either by damage to the radome or other detection techniques used to identify the pointing and tracks of the dish motion could divulge otherwise sensitive information about the operations and purpose of the organization using the ground station.

Cyber Threat to Confidentiality

The cyber domain can also be used by an attacker to gain access to a ground station and determine the exact locations of the SVs being communicated with by reading such data straight from the positioning and communication equipment attached to ground station computers. This means that even with a protective radome, the confidentiality of the space system movements would be nonexistent. This could impact very important operations by those flying the space system. Say, for example, a SV was being jammed over the same location every time it passed overhead and it was preventing successful mission execution in that area.

The assumption would be the enemy has predicted the path of the SV orbits and just jams when it is overhead. If the operators were to communicate with that satellite to have it alter course slightly in an effort to avoid the jamming, the information the ground station used to track and communicate with it on the next pass would reveal the new orbit information to the attacker who has compromised the ground station and could be used to reposition jamming resources. There are obviously other ways of locating the satellite via radar and other technologies, but this example nonetheless shows a way that confidentiality of flight operations can be compromised.

Integrity

Maintaining the integrity of space operations refers to the ability to guarantee that interactions and commands that come from a particular ground station are those that are authorized and expected to be coming from that ground station source.

Non-cyber Threat to Integrity

There are numerous non-cyber threats to the integrity of ground station operations. Whether they are the flight operations of the spacecraft, the execution of its payload, or the receipt and dissemination of the space system data, non-cyber threats boil down to physical security. Space operations require difficult training and are conducted by skilled professionals to avoid irreparable damage being done to the SV or its payload from improper commands being sent to and executed by the SV. Any compromise to physical security which protects the consoles used by the space system operators is a risk to the integrity of those operations, and as such physical security must be commensurate with any other efforts to reduce risk to the space system.

Cyber Threat to Integrity

The cyber threat presents itself to ground station operations beginning at the console where an insider threat or a remote attacker may execute commands from the cyber domain. These remote commands are unauthorized just as those that might be run by an adversary who broke through physical security barriers to attempt to alter or compromise space system operations would be. Just as physical security must be used to control who can access control terminals for space systems, the permissions and restrictions of various users on those systems must each maintain appropriate swim lanes within the system so that users can only execute the commands they are knowledgeable on and responsible for. If the same organization houses the ground station, SV flight operations, and payload operations, the users responsible for flying the spacecraft probably don't need permissions to execute commands tasking the payload and vice versa. Controlling these actions via permissions and user account settings as well as keeping up to date on security issues in an effort to avoid unauthorized escalation of privileges via local cyber attack should all be employed to maintain the integrity of ground station space system operations at the terminal or console level.

Availability

In the sense of ground station availability, we are referring to the ability for a particular ground station to be functioning and available to conduct communications with the SV or SVs and perform flight and/or payload operations. While individual ground stations obviously need to prepare and protect themselves from instances and scenarios that could result in them being unavailable, the space system as a whole should be planned with enough ground stations and even SVs to get to an acceptable level of availability and risk to availability relevant to the mission at hand. In many instances the number of ground stations required will be determine by the need for redundant communications from the ground to space and vice versa over the course of the space system operational life span. One good thing is that, with enough money and resources, new ground stations can be built in new locations if they become necessary or available to increase coverage on the ground just as more SVs can be added to a constellation or a mesh to accomplish similar improvement.

Non-cyber Threat to Availability

The non-cyber threat once again boils down to the physical environment around the ground station. This means planning ground station locations not only to allow for sufficient communications with the SVs as they orbit but also to avoid potentially hazardous environments and locations with likely natural disasters. Additionally, another consideration for ground station location should be protectability. Many space systems are operated by military or defense organizations and serve warfighting and intelligence-gathering activities. Beyond that, many civilian-utilized space systems enable search and rescue, emergency communications, and other vital assets. If the ground station is located in an area where protection from adversaries isn't available, then the ground station operations, at least from that particular ground station, will remain at an elevated risk level.

Cyber Threat to Availability

The cyber domain–based attacks that could impact or negate ground station operations are only limited by the imagination, resources, and access of the attacker. The ground station side of space system operations is the most accessible attack surface to cyber attack, and though it has the greatest access to security capabilities, it poses the most significant impediment to a strong risk posture. An adversary could leverage a cyber attack against many different supporting systems to reduce the availability of a ground station to the overall space system. An attacker could breach the fire prevention and control system of a building and make it think there is a fire in the operations room, soaking the computer systems of the ground station in water and damaging them severely. The attacker could attack the heating, ventilation and air conditioning (HVAC) systems of the building housing computing equipment and crank up the heat in hopes of damaging the ground station equipment that way; power sources to the building running the space operations equipment could be disabled via cyber attack. These and other support systems that have impact on availability of a space system are not as likely to get the cybersecurity focus that, say, control terminals for the flight and payload computers might, and this is a huge potential blind spot in the security posture of a space system that must be addressed with the same scrutiny as the easily identifiable, directly space system tied, computer equipment because the effect can be the same or worse in efforts to compromise them and ultimately compromise space system availability.

Analysis and Dissemination

Access and dissemination are two of the main actions necessary to get space system-provided data to the ultimate customers in a timely manner and usable format. Even though a SV may execute tasking and return the resulting data to Earth as expected by the operators of that space system, it does not necessarily mean that the data is yet useful. Analysis, characterization, or other postprocessing of payload data may be necessary before the data from a SV is in a form that justifies its operations. This also means that any impact to confidentiality, integrity, or appropriately timely availability of that data to customers via the analysis and dissemination process is just as almost as important to the overall mission involved as the hardware flying in space doing executing the mission tasks.

Confidentiality

The confidentiality of the analysis and operational vector involves the analysis and dissemination processes wherein an individual without appropriate need for potentially sensitive data could potentially get unauthorized or accidental access to it. During analysis this could mean that an individual uninvolved in the exploitation of raw SV data was able to view and understand it without having an operational need to do so. The impacts of this can be anywhere from essentially negligible to extremely damaging to national security or competitive operations.

If the breach of confidentiality happens during the dissemination process, it could mean that reporting based on the data from the SV was analyzed and sent to the wrong party that doesn't need to see such information. There also exists a problem where dissemination of analyzed and prepared data may involve reporting off SV data that does not sufficiently obscure the method of collection. The ultimate customers of space system–sourced information may not have any nor should have any idea of the method from which the SV collected certain information. Where this is the case or that collection method is extremely sensitive, the analysis and dissemination processes must closely control what information makes it to external customers to avoid incriminating or revealing sensitive SV capabilities.

Non-cyber Threat to Confidentiality

In a non-cyber attack example, the issue of improper dissemination can be as simple as mislabeling disseminated information with the wrong classification or sensitivity or handling instructions which could result in unauthorized individuals gaining access to data they should not because those handling the mislabeled data are protecting it based on inappropriate dissemination rules. Mischaracterization aside there is also a potential for mistakes to result in data being sent to the wrong individuals via data streams or even emails. In such an instance, if someone without a need to know or appropriate clearance received the data, there would be a breach in the appropriate confidentiality of that data, but at least that person could be informed of how to properly protect and handle such information after the fact due to it being labeled appropriate but sent to an unauthorized person.

Cyber Threat to Confidentiality

Via a cyber attack, a remote malicious actor may be able to compromise the workstations where analysis is conducted and gain access to either raw data from the SV or data that has very specific dissemination controls. In either case this access to the workstation and likely exfiltration of sensitive data to adversary networks represent a loss of that data's confidentiality and illustrate that many devices involved in a space system operational pipeline can impact even the SV. As we discussed, raw or improperly characterized information from the SV might reveal how it is actually collecting that data. If an adversary or competitor were to get that information via a cyber exploitation and exfiltration, they could all together avoid the SV capabilities that target them which essentially makes portions or the entirety of a given mission forfeit.

Integrity

The integrity of data at this phase of space system operations is maintained by ensuring the data that makes it down from the satellite and is analyzed before being sent out correctly represents whatever the original target of that collection may have been. If the payload had a mission to take pictures of a certain place on Earth, analysis should not alter that data in a way that misrepresents what is in truth actually on the ground at that terrestrial location. To do so would violate the integrity of that data.

Non-cyber Threat to Integrity

In many forms of analysis of collected data, specifically imagery or video data, whether from a space collection asset or one on Earth, a human is often involved in identifying objects within that image or video. Though there have been advances in machine learning and artificial intelligence to help aid such determinations, the final decision of what is being seen in the image often comes down to being made by or verified by human eyes. This means that there is still room for error. If a human analyst mischaracterizes an image as something it is not and then passes that information on for dissemination, the integrity of the space systems final product cannot be maintained. This could be as innocuous a mistake as incorrectly identifying a geologic land feature while passing satellite imagery off to topographers to utilize in mapping to something as dire as mistaking a minivan for a tank when passing off targeting imagery to an artillery battery. Once again, though far down the chain from the actual SV taking the images, these types of mistakes can impact the overall perceived effectiveness and accuracy of the space system itself and its mission.

Cyber Threat to Integrity

Unfortunately, with the preceding analytics often taking place on a computer, there is attack surface open to hackers to gain access and alter the resulting data that gets sent for dissemination. If you remember when we talked about threats to sensing payloads, there are two ways that remote exploitation and code execution that change these systems can impact the end product. First an attacker could alter the raw files before the analyst got and reviewed them to say hide something like a dank by changing the pixels that show the tank to match those of the terrain around it. The other method involves altering the reporting after the analyst reviews it to change their determinations. Either way the integrity of disseminated analyzed data would lack integrity and be unreliable or misleading.

Availability

Availability at this stage of the operational vector refers to the availability of that SV data on the ground both for analysis by analysts and dissemination by whatever mediums are to be used. A lack of availability here means that the analysts lose the ability to work at data sets to make determinations and/or that characterized and labeled data then becomes unavailable for dissemination.

Non-cyber Threat to Availability

Any number of things can happen to limit the ability for analysts to continue accessing available raw data from a space system and ultimately hand it off for dissemination. It is unlikely that the ground station that pulls signals down is in the same room or even building where analysis of that data may take place and something as simple as a cut fiber line between said buildings could eliminate the availability of that data for analysis for long periods of time. Even in a situation where backup communication methods or hand couriering data is an option in emergency, it may affect the timeliness of data, and if that data is involved in a military operation or search and rescue, it might not meet mission requirements for relevance due to its age once analyzed.

Cyber Threat to Availability

Raw data from a SV and analyzed data waiting to be disseminated are likely to be data at rest for some amount of time along the way, and this data at rest is another way an attacker can go after the availability of space system information. The installation of malware that deletes certain types of files such as images or corrupts entire databases all together could set back the ultimate production of SV data used by customers for hours, days, or weeks. Each step along the path from download from the SV to analysis and dissemination includes locations where the data is stored on a hard drive and can be deleted by a cyber attacker with enough access. Again, if the space system as a whole is not producing data because it was deleted somewhere along the way before being disseminated out of the space system organization, then the overall mission of the space system is being strategically impacted in a similar fashion to if the SV itself had physical damage impeding payload execution.

Consumers

The last operational vector I will cover are the consumers of space system data. It may seem odd to include consumers as one of the vectors that could be utilized to manifest an impact on the space system. However, without appropriate controls, validation, and monitoring of the data consumers submit to SV operators, there are many risks to the confidentiality of that space system data, its integrity, and ultimately the availability of relevant data in the products the space system produces.

Confidentiality

Confidentiality here is similar to that involving analysis and dissemination, but the source of the issue is instead the consumer and not those performing analysis and dissemination of space system data. In some of these cases, this breach of confidentiality also requires some complacency or lack of attention to detail by members of the space system operational organization as well.

Non-cyber Threat to Confidentiality

Just because consumers are asked to request SV collection in a certain way and to follow certain rules in doing so does not necessarily mean that the human beings doing the consuming follow those rules 100% of the time or don't make mistakes or purposefully inappropriate requests. When an inappropriate request is made from a consumer and goes improperly verified by the space system, it could result in a product being returned to the consumer that gives them information they are not supposed to know, or which is illegal or sensitive. Imagine someone who had access to request collection from an imagery satellite was tasking the satellite to take pictures of his or her vacation home instead of the targets they were authorized to ask collection of photos on. This would be a break of confidentiality of the data the space system can produce by essentially requesting unauthorized information from the space system.

Cyber Threat to Confidentiality

In a similar but cyber-based compromise of the requesting process, a cyber domain–based attacker may be able to get access to unauthorized collection from a SV by exploiting the systems of one of the organizations that consumes its data and not have to go after any system under the operating organization at all. In this situation the hacker has violated the confidentiality of the system by breaching the expected privacy or control of data that gets sent to consumers. This is done by inserting him- or herself using interactive access gained on a computing system at the consumer organization to ask their own tasking of the SV. This could be to simply gain intelligence via the payload mission method on the SV or gain information about that actual payload's capabilities.

Integrity

Both the cyber and non-cyber examples for confidentiality of information being requested for collection by the consumer organization also represent a compromise in the space systems integrity via the consumer organization. Improper or unauthorized requests for collection, whether they make it through to actual execution or not, are all risks to the integrity of data produced by a space system. If it became known that a space system could not guarantee that the data it was requested to gather was of an authorized and legal manner, it could result in the space system being shut down or operations put on freeze until security and procedural changes could once again ensure the integrity of tasking the space system was both receiving and ultimately executing.

Availability

Availability at the consumer level is the last stop for data from a SV and the last opportunity for the productivity of the space system to be impacted by risks to the availability of the data it produces for those customers. No matter how successful and regimented the space system operations are, a sufficient impact to consumer organizations could lead them to stop participating in or sponsoring such space systems in the future because of a lack of cost benefit via the products they are unable to receive.

Non-cyber Threat to Availability

Depending on the space system or systems involved, there is likely to be a question of prioritization. SVs are expensive and often perform important missions for consumers on the ground. Take an imagery satellite, for example, that takes pictures over a particular area of interest. The consumer base for such a system might be multiple government organizations, military units, and intelligence functions. This is the same of a civilian space asset that takes imagery. Such imagery could be useful to anyone from farmers to law enforcement or even surveyors and map makers. Adequately prioritizing the collection tasked to either of these imaging satellite examples should be done in a way that produces the most cost benefit overall in many cases.

This might mean that a farmer rarely gets priority to have pictures taken if law enforcement use is heavy during a certain period. It could also mean that certain military units never get images from a satellite because an important intelligence mission is ongoing. In either case and no matter how this tasking is prioritized, there is potential that the SV may be essentially unavailable to some of the customers to task and that some may almost always have priority. There are chances that choices to build more ground stations or launch more satellites could mitigate such an issue, but when that is not an option, availability concerns for all consumers will have to be balanced by a third party or perhaps the space system organization itself to attempt to optimize availability.

Cyber Threat to Availability

From a cyber perspective, the need for adequate prioritization of consumer collection tasking to enable successful availability of a space system to all consumers affords one last attack surface from which the cyber domain could lead to an impact to the space system by preventing one or more customers from getting the data they need. Malware could be used to alter tasking requests from a certain consumer after they are written to lower the labeled prioritization such that they never end up getting processed by the space system itself. In situations where a third-party organization handles prioritization and ordering of tasking from multiple consumers to a space system, that organization itself is also a target adversary hacker could seek to exploit and attack.

Conclusion

The takeaway from this chapter should be that the totality of attack vectors a space system is exposed to, which ultimately affects its ability to be successful or be perceived as successful, is extremely diverse within the operational entities that make up the space system. Further even at the consumer sites, there is risk represented by various attack surfaces that can allow for impact to the space system itself. Even though software and solutions exist to optimize and validate tasking and execution of SV tasks, an adequately informed and resourced attacker would be able to find ways around such measures. Internet-facing web sites have long faced such issues when it comes to taking input and validating it before passing it to the back end to avoid exploitation. Space system tasking software is simply a tailored and specific input system, likely facing less security scrutiny, and poses a similar risk to the eventual ultimate back end, which is in this case expensive and valuable SVs.

CHAPTER 10

Compromise Microanalysis

To really hammer home how real the threat to space systems is, I wanted to step through a detailed example of a compromise originating with the targeting of program at a high level and ending with an impacted space vehicle (SV). To make this as relevant as possible, I am also going to include example operating systems and software used in various Internet of Things (IOT) devices and space systems as well. I will cover which exploits or techniques could actually be used to compromise those systems and will do my best to keep the targets as timely and relevant as possible.

If for some reason you are reading this book many years after I wrote it and criticize the datedness of technologies or software, understand that this chapter and the example targets and exploits herein were researched and written about in December 2019. I would also point out that to date many servers and workstations, especially those involved in space, still leverage nearly 20-year-old operating systems such as Microsoft Windows Server 2000 or 2003 and Windows XP.

The following example is not representative of any particular space system I have come across or researched and should not be seen as a how-to guide on hacking into a specific system. I will also say that I will not cover the attack process in its totality because having once been a professional ethical hacker and not wanting to encourage unprofessional behavior, I may leave out or alter certain details of the compromise process. This is intentional. What is important to take away from the following example is that space systems such as those that include small satellites can be compromised, today, right now, and that the cybersecurity and space industries are currently behind the power curve when you consider what is available through open source research on the Internet in regard to attack tools.

© Jacob G. Oakley 2020
J. G. Oakley, *Cybersecurity for Space*, https://doi.org/10.1007/978-1-4842-5732-6_10

A Series of Unfortunate Events

Without further delay let's get into the chain of events that could lead to the compromise and ultimately the death of a space system operation.

The Plan

Firstly, we will set a realistic stage for these events to play out in. After all, before we attack a space system and ultimately the SV it operates, we need to know why. Let's say a nation state has decided to sponsor a cyber attack campaign against an academic space system as a proof of concept and learning evolution for potential follow-on militarized cyber domain actions. This way the target is likely a softer one, without classified or sensitive systems and some of the added protections they might come with. Additionally, since the targets are not military in nature, it will be viewed less as an act of war if the activity was somehow attributed by the targeted academic institution or host country. Lastly, there is the added benefit that many academic institutions work hand in hand with the defense sectors of many countries' governments, and tactics, tools, and procedures learned and utilized against the test target could be rolled into actual operations.

Targeting

To determine the target for a scenario like this, which will be used as a proof of concept, the nation state is likely to let the target identify itself. This is done by simply picking what looks like the lowest hanging fruit; instead of an actual cyber operation which may have determined the target first and approached attack avenues after, here the attack avenues choose the target for ease of exploitation. So the attacker will canvass the Internet for academic instructions announcing their first ever space and small satellite programs which have recently or will soon launch their SV. This way the target set includes only institutions new at space and small satellite development and likely to make more mistakes than those with established programs.

Once the institution is identified, the attacker can canvass social media and the institutions' web sites and other locations like LinkedIn or GitHub for those students who will be involved in the program, specifically those who are likely to be involved in writing or uploading code such as electrical engineers and computer science students. Once a target individual is picked, the attacker can research what projects and collaborations the student has been involved in. Then, creating a fake persona that looks like it is an academic within a related field from a prestigious university who wants help or to collaborate on something since they read the target's work and were obviously thoroughly impressed.

Personal Computer

The first step in the actual exploit and compromise purpose is to gain access and privileges to the personal computers of the target individual within the target institution.

How

Once the right individual has been selected for targeting, the attacker can use the fake persona from the prestigious academic university to build a rapport with the target and eventually use that rapport to get him or her to open files that contain malware which when executed give the attacker remote access to the target's personal laptop. There are many ways to abuse a social relationship to get a target to execute something, but some common and relevant methods could be using macros within a Microsoft Word document or PDF. Once that document is opened and a pop-up is clicked (at the instruction of the attacker), malicious code is now running with the context of that user, and one of any number of privilege escalation techniques can be used to gain system access and further implant backdoors and other malware on the target's personal laptop, as shown in Figure 10-1.

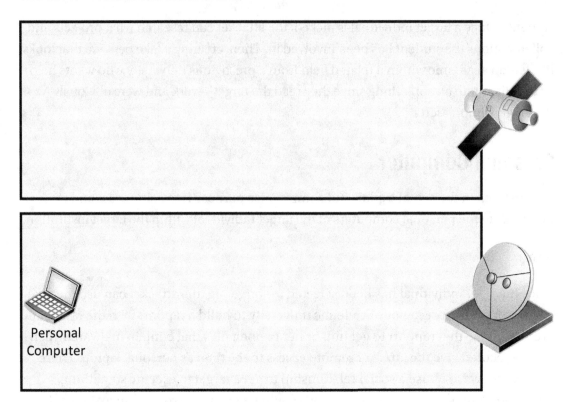

Figure 10-1. *Access to Personal Computer*

Why

Besides gaining an initial cyber foothold in the target space related to the institution and its space program, access to install malware on this personal computer has other opportunities beyond enabling deeper access into the organization and its computers. Installing keyloggers and applications that record off the laptop's microphone can also enable the attackers to gain further intelligence about the individual and the organization and its space program. This could be used to tailor further social engineering attacks against other members of the organization or to glean engineering and operational details that the target talks or types about.

Phone

With access to the personal laptop gained, the attacker will look to exploit something like a personal phone as that sort of device is more likely to be taken into areas of interest than a laptop. In cases where both are taken to areas where space system work is done, then the attacker has simply doubled his or her access.

How

With system-level access to a Microsoft Windows personal computer, there are any number of ways to exploit and gain access to the devices such as smart phones which get plugged in for charging and file movement purposes. To cite a specific example, there is a Windows executable Trojan called DualToy[1] described and reported on by Paolo Alto in 2016 which allows for the loading of malicious applications and their code via USB charging cable connections and relying on already established android smart phone to Windows computer profile relationships. This would allow the attacker to backdoor and install toolkits and malware on the phone as necessary; the movement of the attacker's access is shown in Figure 10-2.

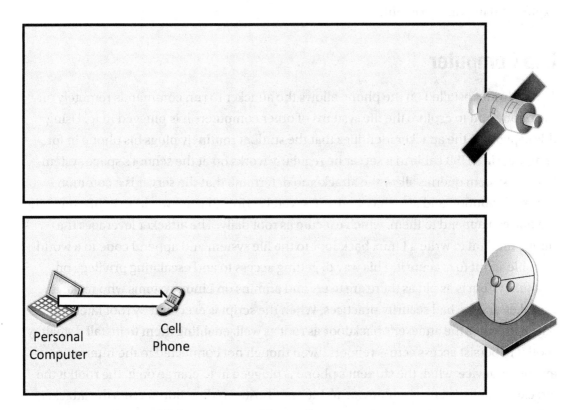

Figure 10-2. *Personal Computer to Phone Compromise*

---

[1]https://unit42.paloaltonetworks.com/dualtoy-new-windows-trojan-sideloads-risky-apps-to-android-and-ios-devices/

Why

The initial purpose of this exploitation is to pivot to a device in the smart phone which is more likely to be brought near and connected to the networks and computers of the space system. There is the added benefit of providing further situational awareness and personal connections as well as emails, text, and phone conversations between the initial target and other members of the team. Even if the smart phone never got connected to further target space, the microphone on board could be used to gather intelligence by collecting conversations in the space system lab area. Thanks to the Internet connectivity of smart phones, if plugged into something like an air-gapped network used for ground station operations, it can act as an exfiltration and remote exploit and interaction enabler.

Lab Computer

The malware installed on the phone allows the attacker to run commands remotely on the phone and to explore the file systems of other computers it is plugged in to. Using this capability, the attacker identifies that the student routinely plugs his phone in for charging via a USB cable to a server he regularly works on at the school's space system lab. File system queries allow the attacker to determine that the server is a common Linux distribution and also that there are several scripts that are world writable, meaning anyone can append to them, which execute as root daily. The attacker leverages the phone implant to write a Linux backdoor to the file system and append code to a world writable script to execute it. This way of getting access to and escalating privilege on a Linux system is as old as there are users and admins on Linux systems who make mistakes or have bad security practices. When the script is executed by root later that day, it executes the attacker's backdoor as root as well, enabling them to install a stealthy rootkit to persist access across reboots. Even though not connected to the Internet or any other device, when the student's phone is plugged in to charge on it, the rootkit the attacker installed can communicate to Internet-hosted redirection servers the attacker utilizes to obfuscate their location and task the implants in this compromise chain.

How

Figure 10-3 shows the next pivot the attacker will make to the lab server hosting virtual machines.

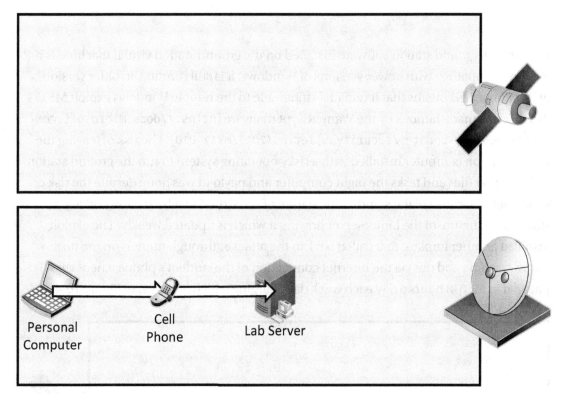

Figure 10-3. *Phone to Lab Server*

Why

This lab server will be used by the attacker to go after and exploit the ground station virtual machine computer that is hosted on it. The ground station computer does not communicate to any external network; however, it does have a local area network it communicates with only the host computer on. This means that the only way to exploit it is from the lab server which hosts it. If this ends up being possible, the lab server serves as a path back to the exfiltration potential utilized via tools installed on the student's phone. Additionally when files are brought back from the satellite, they are copied to the lab server as a backup so the attacker can now see what the satellite does as well as its raw collection from its payload.

Ground Station Computer

Security on the ground station is essentially the last layer of defense in depth protecting the satellite. Tasking from the ground is inherently trusted by the SV, and it affords attackers the most reasonable way to attack the SV components.

How

Because the ground station software installed on the ground station virtual machine is not forward compatible with newer versions of Windows, it is still running an older version of Windows. This means that it remains vulnerable to the remote Windows exploit MS17-010 that was made famous by the WannaCrypt malware (https://docs.microsoft.com/en-us/security-updates/securitybulletins/2017/ms17-010). The risk of leaving the ground station computer installed with a risky operating system to run the ground station software that flies and tasks the flight computer and payload was done despite the risk of exploitation because of the stand-alone nature of the virtual machine it runs on and the stand-alone nature of the Linux server hosting it which is updated weekly. The exploit installed another implant that called back to the attacker through tunnels on the host Linux machine and out via the Internet connection of the student's phone whenever it is plugged in for 6–8 hours a day each week day charging which is shown in Figure 10-4.

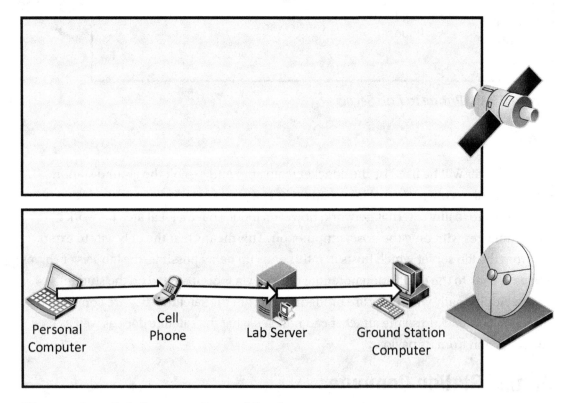

Figure 10-4. *Lab Server to Ground Station*

Why

Very simply the ground station is exploited to enable the eventual exploitation and/or unauthorized tasking of the SV itself.

Payload Computer

The first computing device on board the SV that the attackers are going to target is the payload computer since it takes very straightforward tasking from the ground station to include software and operating system updates. Additionally, altering behavior of the payload computer and/or its code will not result in immediately noticeable effects by those operating the space system as the attacker learns the rest of the attack surface on board. So long as the attacker allows the payload to continue carrying out the tasks those on the ground expect, any additional malicious activities are not likely to be noticed.

How

Legitimate commands are utilized to tell the payload to upload a software update which contains malware that when executed will overwrite the backup images of the operating system copies of those operating systems that also contain malware so that it will be persisted through reimaging of the payload computer operating system. This malware also looks for tasking in legitimate payload tasking files which the attacker uses metadata sections of the file to input tasking hidden from the space system operators. Evidence of both of these actions are deleted from logs on both the SV and the ground station as are artifacts of the malicious activity, and the attacker now has access to the SV which is shown in Figure 10-5.

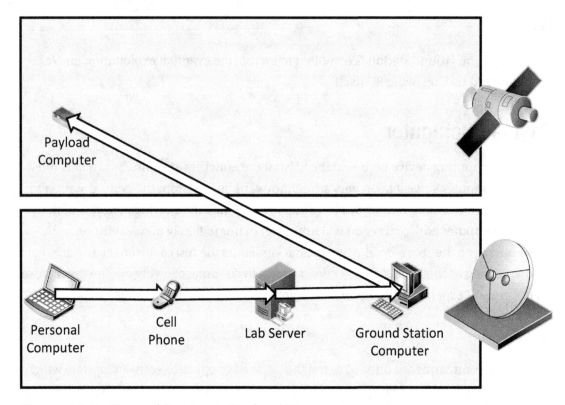

Figure 10-5. *Ground Station to Payload Computer*

Why

There is malware installed on the SV payload computer which is persisted and receives and executes tasking in the privileged context from the malware installed on the ground station via infected payload tasking files. The information gained via this implant are downloaded as what appear to be corrupt copies of good image files from the payload computer which as soon as they reach the ground station are copied to another location so that when the space system operators delete the unusable image file, the data from the SV payload computer implant is maintained. This data is then sent by the ground station implant through tunnels on the host operating system out to the attacker's server on the Internet where they can create new payload computer implant tasking and upload it via the same channels.

Data Handler

Scans run by the payload implant reveal the presence of a C&DH computer which is responsible for watchdog, health, and maintenance functions for the rest of the spacecraft and is likely what talks to the software defined radio which the attacker intends to eventually leverage to kill the satellite.

How

The data handler is running a current year version of VxWorks which in 2018–2019 had many vulnerabilities disclosed to include some six which would enable remote code execution.[2] One of these is leveraged by an executable sent up to the implant in the payload computer and executed. The vulnerability can be used to execute commands which enumerate the data handler computer and send the data back to the payload computer implant for eventual download and passage over the attacker communication channels, which are illustrated in Figure 10-6.

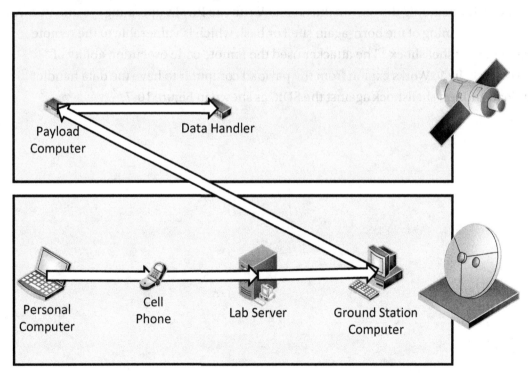

Figure 10-6. Payload Computer to Data Handler

---

[2]https://its.ny.gov/security-advisory/multiple-vulnerabilities-wind

Why

With the ability to execute remote code at will on the data handler, the attacker can determine the location presence and location of watchdog scripts that may execute in attempts to save the SV from issues malicious or otherwise. Access to code execution on the data handler computer also allows the attacker to determine the operating system of the software defined radio which controls communications to the ground station.

SDR

The piece of computing equipment which allows the SV to communicate with the ground station is the SDR, and compromise of it and execution of malicious code could prevent any further communication to it.

How

Some SDRs including the one on the target SV run the POSIX operating system. POSIX allows for running of the born-again shell or bash which is vulnerable to the remote vulnerability shellshock.[3] The attacker used the remote code execution ability of leveraging the VxWorks exploit from the payload computer to have the data handler upload and run shellshock against the SDR, as shown in Figure 10-7.

---

[3]https://blog.cloudflare.com/inside-shellshock/

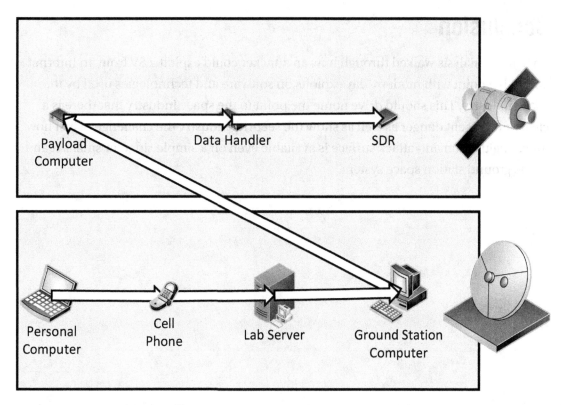

Figure 10-7. *Data Handler to SDR*

Why

With access to execute code on the SDR, the attacker can then tell it to listen and communicate on a completely different frequency than the ground station expects. This way, each time the satellite makes a pass within view of the ground station, it is not listening on the frequency which the ground station is using to hail it so it will never respond. The access to the data handler was used to disable watchdog scripts that might trigger after so many passes without hearing from a ground station, and encryption keys are overwritten with useless data from the communications stack for good measure. The attackers have now essentially killed the SV.

Conclusion

This microanalysis walked through how an attacker could exploit a SV from an Internet accessible point with modern-day exploits on software and technologies used by the space industry. This should drive home the point to the space industry that there is a clear and present danger as well as show the security industry the challenge of just how much digitization and attack surface is available even on a simple singular smallsat and single ground station space system.

CHAPTER 11

Compromise Macroanalysis

Walking through the compromise of a single ground station and space vehicle (SV) as well as their component devices certainly drives home the real threat at a system level. To further present just how impactful compromise of and via a SV can be, we will now proceed through a scenario that provides a macroanalysis of an example widespread and far-reaching space system compromise. The following will build on the walk-through before and reference some of the cyber techniques that were used and incorporate them at a higher level. This macroanalysis will not delve into as many technical details and is more aimed at tying together just how prolific space system compromises could be.

As a society we are continuously increasingly dependent on space systems to enable our day-to-day activities and communications. Military and governments as well as most industries rely on space systems, especially communication and positioning systems, and their operations would be crippled temporarily if not permanently if certain space systems were to fail. Imagine that the following is a cyber campaign by the same organization that attacked the school, leveraging lessons learned to go after a larger organization with multiple ground stations and multiple SVs. Additionally this space system has physically dispersed ground stations and separate organizations that conduct flight operations for the satelli;te and another which handles payload operations, each from their own sets of ground station sites.

Initial Ground Station

Once again, the initial foothold in the space system will be obtained through compromise of a ground station. In this situation I will give an example of how a ground station might be compromised directly and not involved multiple exploitations of personal devices to get to and maintain connectivity of a hacked ground station server.

141

© Jacob G. Oakley 2020
J. G. Oakley, *Cybersecurity for Space*, https://doi.org/10.1007/978-1-4842-5732-6_11

How

In this scenario the ground station server was the victim of interdiction. When the device was at the company responsible for integrating the SDR, antennas, and encryption devices to the SV, a malicious insider installed a hardware backdoor hidden in a swapped-in DVD drive, allowing communications over a cellular network connection. Figure 11-1 shows the system of systems view of the overall space system.

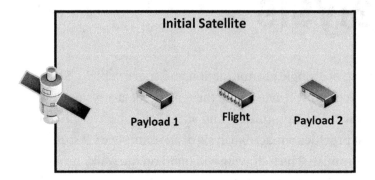 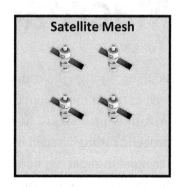

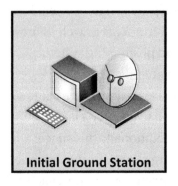  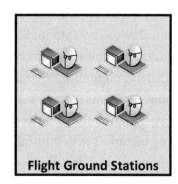

Figure 11-1. *Scenario Diagram*

Why

This implant allows the attacker constant communications to and from the ground station whenever necessary. This access will be used by the attacker to target the space system, upload malicious code and binaries, as well as exfiltrate data from the space system in a nearly undetectable manner.

Payload 1 Computer

This particular SV is a member of a mesh, and as such it has a payload that performs a mission such as imagery as well as a payload that enables communications across the mesh of SVs. The imaging payload will be referred to as payload 1 and similar to our microanalysis will be used as the initial target for exploitation via the compromised ground station. The attacker is also best served to go after the imaging payload computer since the compromised ground station belongs to the organization that tasks and operates the imaging payloads, not the one which flies the satellites and monitors telemetry.

How

The attacker can gain remote code execution on the SV by utilizing infected tasking files that the SV ingests automatically. The attacker does not need to immediately leverage something like a code vulnerability to get arbitrary execution on the first target computing device on board the SV. This initial exploitation from the ground into the SV is shown in Figure 11-2.

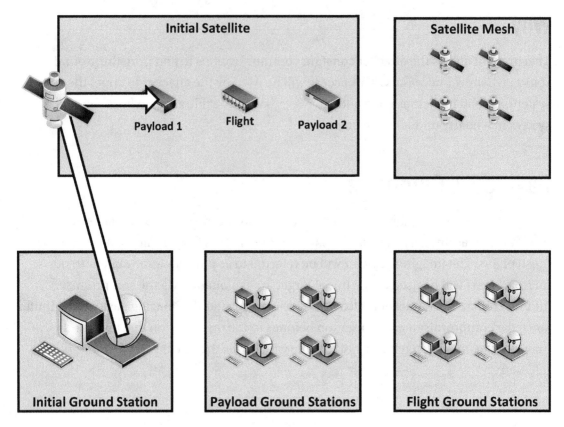

Figure 11-2. *Payload 1 Computer Compromised*

Why

Using the infected tasking files to gain execution, the attackers can implant their malicious tools into the payload 1 computer and use it as a foothold for further situational awareness and exploitation within the SV.

Payload Ground Network

Now the attacker has initial access to the SV maintained. Communications from the attacker's malware connect back from the SV during passes, through the implant on the ground station server and ultimately back to wherever the hacker is ultimately located.

How

In the same way that tasking files can be infected with malware and sent up to the SV to be executed, collection files can be similarly modified to allow the compromised SV to act as a launch point for malware downloads to other ground stations that the SV flies over. In this way a compromised payload computer on a satellite could be used to infect multiple separate and unconnected ground sites that download mission data from that payload. This next phase of the campaign is shown in Figure 11-3.

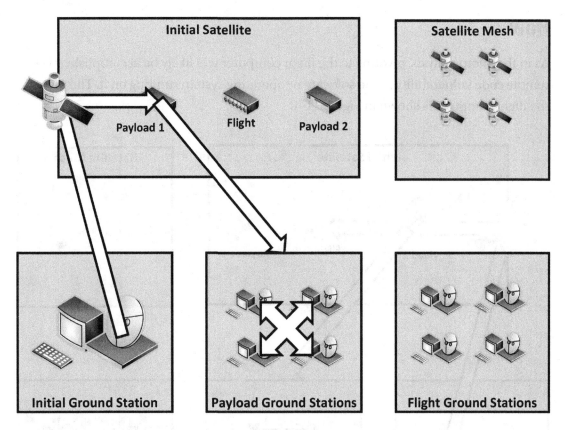

Figure 11-3.   *Payload Ground Stations Compromised*

Why

With access enabled to multiple ground stations operating the payloads, the attacker now has the ability to maintain separate lines of access to the SV. With more ground station access, the attacker will also have more numerous communications windows

145

with the SV as it passes over the now numerous compromised ground sites operating and tasking the imaging payload. Additionally, it means that any malicious activities the attacker may conduct can affect a larger portion of the total space system.

Flight Computer

With more persistent access to the space system across the payload ground station, the attacker will turn to pivoting on to the flight computer.

How

As in the microanalysis, pivoting to the flight computer will likely be accomplished via remote code vulnerability in the software or operating system running on it. The pivot to the flight computer is shown in Figure 11-4.

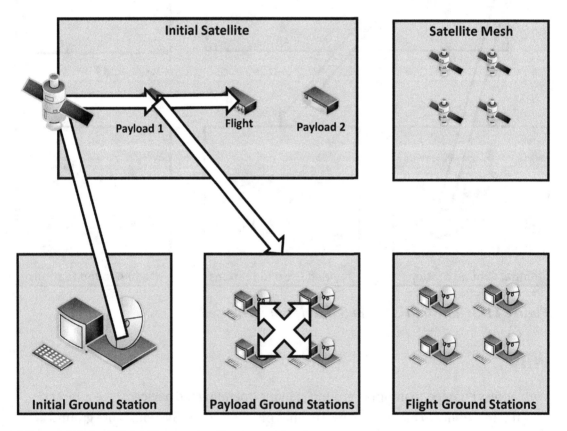

Figure 11-4. *Flight Computer Compromised*

Why

In this particular SV, the flight computer is actually a beefed-up version which not only handles telemetry and manipulating the SV flight hardware but also handles communications via the SDR and encryption to establish downlinks to the ground stations which actually fly the satellite.

Flight Ground Network

Just as the payload operations are conducted from a multitude of ground stations to support the mesh operations, so too do the flight operations. Flying a mesh of many satellites would require access via several physically diverse ground stations to maximize the utilization of and benefit from having many SVs in several orbital planes all running missions and downloading the resulting data. Making sure these satellites stay in the correct orbits and maximize persistence for the payload operations requires a network of ground stations performing flying the mesh.

How

In the same way the payload data was used to infect the payload ground stations with malware, telemetry files from the flight computer can provide the same attack vector to the flight ground stations. When they ingest and process telemetry data on operations console, they become infected with backdoors which also try to communicate out to the Internet. This compromise of the flight ground sites is shown in Figure 11-5.

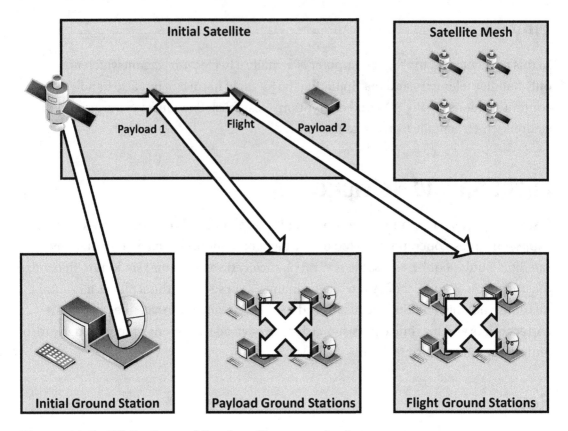

Figure 11-5. *Flight Ground Stations Compromised*

Why

Access to the ground network used to fly the satellites will be more useful to the attackers as they consider performing attack actions on the mesh as the flight operators are more likely to be the ones trying to regain access to the SVs in the event of some cyber-induced effect. The added ground networks also give the attacker even more access to the compromised SV and added persistence.

Payload 2 Computer

While compromise of additional SVs is certainly possible from either of the compromised ground networks used for payload tasking and flight, the attackers want to explore attacking the mesh from space. To do this they need to gain access to payload 2 computer which operates the communications, routing, and switching of data across the mesh of SV crosslinks.

How

Using the flight computer, which provides an interface to the secondary payload, the attacker can once again use a remote code execution vulnerability to pivot to the mesh communication payload. This is shown in Figure 11-6.

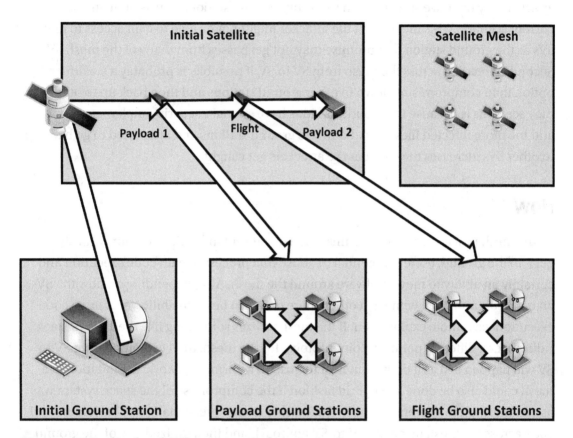

Figure 11-6. *Payload 2 Computer Compromised*

Why

This payload 2 computer will provide the final launch point from which the attacker will pivot into the other SVs within the mesh.

Mesh

Once the attacker has gained access to the payload 2 computer, it is time to explore options on how to proliferate access across the mesh. Infecting other SVs from the initially compromised one is valuable to an attacker for a couple reasons. First, the attacker may not have spread down to various ground stations as was done in our current scenario. This means that the attacker might not be able to gain access to many SVs as the ground station compromise may not get passes from many of the mesh SVs. Second, spreading across the mesh from SV to SV, if possible, is probably a stealthier option than compromising down to other ground stations and then back up to other SVs they see. This is because the ground stations have stronger security implementations, and the more infected files passed down to ground stations and attempted to go back up to other SVs increases the chances the attackers get caught.

How

As the mesh processes and moves mission data around in an effort to more quickly get it to the ground, there is potential to abuse that process to gain code execution and certainly an ability to move malware around the mesh. Also, depending on how the SVs actually communicate with each other, there may also be a possibility for remote code execution via remote exploitation. If the mesh utilizes something like the TCP/IP stack riding over a different point-to-point protocol for the mesh, then exploiting from SV to SV will happen just as it does from host to host on a normal network. Exploitation of a mesh could also be done in a hybrid fashion if the compromise of the space system was as complete as our current example. An attacker could spread malicious backdoors and code across the mesh using the SV-to-SV approach and then utilized one of the ground station networks to execute those files by saying they are an update to a driver or any other number of ways. This final compromise of the mesh is shown in Figure 11-7.

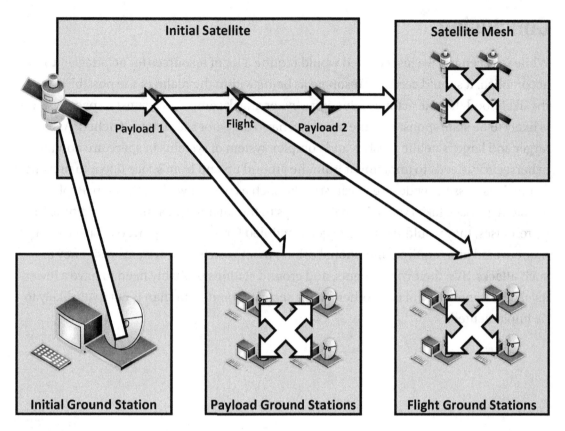

Figure 11-7. *Mesh Compromised*

Why

With the SVs, flight ground stations, and payload ground stations all compromised, an attacker could launch an attack to kill the entire space system in such a way that there is little or no ability for the operators to respond or recover. Using the same attack from the microanalysis example of disabling communications by attacking the SDR, the attacker could proliferate the attack binary and execute it in tandem on all SVs across the mesh. At the same time, repurposed ransomware akin to the WannaCrypt attack can be used to encrypt the hard drives of the computers in both the flight and payload operations' ground networks. With no intention of unencrypting the hard drives or even receiving the ransomware payment, the attacker will set the space system organization down a rabbit chase, thinking they were only the victim of a terrestrial network attack. By the time they recovered their ground networks, it would become apparent that the entire mesh in space had gone dark.

Conclusion

While the scenario we just covered would require a lot of resources for an attacker to accomplish, it should certainly resonate as being within the realm of the possible. Given the likelihood that the actor conducting a cyber attack campaign against a space system is likely to be state sponsored, the attack scenario does not seem so far-fetched. As larger and larger satellite meshes and complex system of systems in space are operated, cybersecurity needs to implement from the ground up and from space down to prevent as much as possible widespread catastrophe such as we just walked through. Replacing a system in space takes years. Even if backups to the satellites in a mesh were sitting in warehouses, they would still need to get scheduled for launch, deployed in space, and maneuvered into required operational orbits. To improve space systems resiliency to such attacks, SVs, their components, and ground stations probably need to have a lower level of assumed trust of each other from a security standpoint than is currently likely to be implemented.

CHAPTER 12

Summary

After introducing space systems and the constraints and challenges of operating within the space environment, we covered extensively the threats to space vehicles and their mission. Discussing at length the vectors an attacker might leverage to introduce those threats and then ultimately walking through a pair of scenarios to drive home how the various threats and vectors could be combined in a cyber attack campaign to wreak havoc across a space system and its operations, I would like to now cover some of the cyber problems related to space systems which will need to be acknowledged and addressed by both the space and cybersecurity communities moving forward.

The Cost Problem

Space systems and especially complex space systems involving a mesh of vehicles have a cost problem. By cost I mean that the cost of implementing a fix to a cybersecurity problem is hard to justify to a space system operator as being worth of implementation, if the cost is definable at all. The easiest way to represent such cost to a space system owner or operator is by identifying the amount of their mission window that will be consumed by doing something. That something might be changing a configuration which will have negligible impact to the overall mission life span, or it could be uploading and re-installing a new version of an operating system for a space vehicle resident component.

A configuration change likely has a low size so it doesn't take up much of a pass to upload it to the space vehicle, and implementing the configuration change on the onboard computing device might take only seconds. Conversely re-installing an operating system might take many passes to upload the files necessary. Worse, installation might take a longer period of time and come with the added risk that if there is an issue during the re-install process and probably power cycling of that component, it might stop functioning all together.

© Jacob G. Oakley 2020
J. G. Oakley, *Cybersecurity for Space*, https://doi.org/10.1007/978-1-4842-5732-6_12

Given the latter I think the decision from many system operators would be to accept the risk of someone potentially compromising the component or having an error due to a bug happen than introduce the risk of potentially irreparably damaging the space vehicle during re-install. Since this is the case, as cybersecurity professionals, we need to be able to tell the story to the owner about how the vulnerability or flaw they don't necessarily understand really poses a risk and impact to their space system so they can make better informed decisions.

More difficult than situations where cost is known are the situations where it is not. It is one thing to try and justify taking ten passes to upload a fix and 1 hour of time on the vehicle to install as well as risking a reboot. That would be a situation that can easily be translated into a percentage of space vehicle mission lifetime. It is entirely another thing to try and convince an owner of a space system mesh to roll out an operating system re-install across a mesh of satellites and not be able to communicate what the impact to operations will be.

There is a whole lot more analysis that needs to be done to calculate how long it takes to get something like a driver or an operating system up into one or more space vehicles in the mesh and then proliferate that file across the mesh and install and power cycle the updated component. Coming up with the answer to that problem in a representation of the time it takes and the risk to the various space vehicles as they power cycle is difficult on its own. Then comparing that to the overall operational life span of the mesh and the immediate mission impact of power cycling the devices represents a more complex problem.

In a mesh, is it acceptable if one out of ten satellites to have issues after the power cycle? What about 1 in 100? Optimizing this problem to identify a way to proliferate an update file across a mesh and install and power cycle when various space vehicles are not actively conducting payload mission activity or communicating with a ground station would certainly make the process more appealing to space system owners. That being said, the analysis and problem solving to come up with these methods would require significant investment from skilled space professionals, machine learning, and cybersecurity.

What can't happen is the owner of a large mesh of satellites arguing for not addressing a critical cybersecurity concern because they are willing to assume the risk on the premise that as long as only one or two of their satellites get hacked, they can still operate the mesh and carry out the mission. If a cyber security vulnerability can affect one satellite in a mesh, it can affect all of them and the repercussions of a cyber attack could spread across a mesh of satellites just as quickly as that mesh passes payload mission data around itself and down to the ground.

The Cyber Warfare Problem

Unfortunately for the space domain, it has a big bad boogeyman in cyber warfare and a boogeyman that is exceptionally suited to space domain operations. A quick aside on cyber warfare, it has a cost-benefit problem of its own. Let's say you want to disable an enemy radar site to safely fly a rescue mission into the enemy country. If you wanted to use cyber effects to do so, you have to hope that the site is accessible, and you have the exploits necessary to gain access.

Even assuming that away, a cyber effect against the radar site is not guaranteed to function as intended, and a battle damage assessment of whether or not it worked well enough to completely disable the radar is nearly impossible. The other option is with a kinetic effect where I can just shoot a missile at the radar site whenever I want, observe the crater in the ground where the radar site used to be, and then safely fly over it on my rescue mission. Now, if I was flying the helicopter on that rescue mission, I will be a lot more comfortable flying over the smoking crater of what used to be a radar site than looking at what appears to be an intact radar system thinking to myself, man I hope those cyber nerds did their job.

This is a problem in most warfighting domains, air, land, and sea, for instance, where a kinetic effect often has a much better cost benefit than a cyber one. In space the opposite is true. A kinetic effect against, say, a satellite in space would create a debris field in a popular orbital plane, travelling thousands of miles per hour and potentially destroying unrelated space vehicles belonging to any number of people. The space domain is the perfect place for cyber warfare because if it can be done successfully, a satellite will be disabled quietly on orbit or burn itself up in the atmosphere and pose negligible risk to other space systems.

The other issue for the space domain concerning cyber warfare is that any cyber action taken on a space vehicle is almost sure to be an attack effect that ultimately disables the satellite or its mission capability. Intelligence gathering or even altering of payload mission data is easier to do from a cyber perspective and just as effective if done on a compromised ground station. So the only real reason to go through the trouble of getting code execution on the satellite is to damage or disable it or use it as a launch point to compromise other space vehicles or ground stations.

Tying together the facts that cyber warfare is particularly suited to the space domain and that cyber attacks against a space vehicle are almost certainly in an effort to disable or damage the space system, we come to another frightening conclusion. The most likely individuals to target space systems and the space vehicles that are operated within them are nation state or nation state sponsored actors and advanced persistent threats. This means that the cybersecurity threats posed to most space systems are to a one likely to be highly motivated, highly resourced, and highly skilled.

The Test Problem

Currently, for space specifically, there is a bit of a test problem. Where other environmental and operational risks are both mitigated during design and development as well as exercised, for cyber this is not the case. For the structural integrity of a space vehicle's components, things are done like specifically torquing each bolt to a prescribed amount of torque determined by engineers. After this is done though, the space vehicle is still exercised through a vibration test to ensure that it holds up under the shaking it will experience during launch and deployment.

In some cases, government regulations dictate a validation of security controls on space systems tailored to their being a space vehicle or normal network like a ground station. This is similar to making sure all the bolts have been tightened with the correct amount of torque. The closest thing in the cyber domain to something like a vibration test would be to combine software testing and red teaming to actually exercise the code and computational activities on the space vehicle and ensure they are not easily compromised by an attacker despite having met validation checks of a cybersecurity risk framework. Without both compliance and an exercising of the space vehicle and ground station security apparatus, space systems will have an elevated and partially unknown cyber risk posture.

The Adaptation Problem

All non-cyber risks to a space vehicle can be considered mitigated when appropriate steps are taken to burn down that risk and those steps are verified, validated, and exercised. In the case of risks to the integrity of the space vehicle's physical components, the risk of breaking during launch can be mitigated by appropriate construction and torque definitions and verification that they were followed during the build and validated through being exercised in a vibration test.

At that point the risk can be considered acceptable and that's the end of it. With cybersecurity issues, not only do solutions need to continue to improve but they need to evolve with the threats. A cybersecurity risk mitigation solution for a space vehicle today might be nullified by a different vulnerability and exploit being discovered and weaponized tomorrow. As space systems adapt to cyber threats, those threats are also adapting to overcome the defenses of the space systems. This means that there can be no complacency by space system operators after initial cybersecurity checks are passed.

The Defense in Depth Problem

Another problem with current space system architectures and operations is the overly abundant trust between the systems that make up these systems of systems. It has resulted in most current systems having no defense in depth beyond the ground station. From the ground station up, everything is completely trusted, and the space vehicles and other ground stations trust what they get from each other completely. This is the case because it is more computationally efficient to trust what you are receiving from component to component on a space vehicle as well as from the ground station to the space vehicle and vice versa. This is also the same for mesh communications.

Implementing a little suspicion and verification of what is being passed from component to component and system to system in the space system will go a long way in preventing ease of attack and ease of attack proliferation across space systems. As computational resources on board space vehicles become more powerful, there will be enough resources to perform more permissions and rule-based security, and if a space system can afford the resource cost of implementing security solutions, they should.

The Modernization Problem

The last problem for cyber and space that I want to cover is the modernization problem. This is really manifested in two forms. First there is a need for modernization, and second there is a need to modernize correctly. The need for modernization is because the operating systems and software currently in use by space systems are stripped-down, resource-conscious, power budget–constrained in efforts to squeeze everything possible out of a space vehicle to accomplish the functional mission necessary using as little resources as possible. What this leads to though, is that via a compromised ground station, an attacker is essentially attacking the computing devices of yesteryear which have limited, if any, security implementations with the tools, exploits, and computing power of today.

As onboard computers grow in capability, they will likely transition from running one-off software, tiny and real-time operating systems and begin using more traditional Linux or Unix distributions. This makes it easier on those developing code for space vehicles as their code is more traditional, more portable, and easier to implement. They also get the benefit of having access to much larger communities of support. In general, it is just easier to implement functionality via software from a more modern operating system. While this makes it easier for developers to write code that runs effectively on the space vehicle, it also makes it easier for attackers to write malware that runs effectively on the space vehicle.

As space systems modernize and start using operating systems closer to what is seen in many places terrestrially, the attack surface of space systems will go from foreign to many attackers to familiar. I say this not to dissuade such modernization but to caution that as choices are made to move from something like VxWorks or OpenRTOS to things like CentOS or BSD, the full capability of those operating systems is utilized, not just from an ease of coding and higher functionality standpoint but also to leverage the more mature security solutions available to such operating systems like stateful software firewalls, mature permissions management, and the like.

The danger is that to make development of a space vehicle easier, the choice is made to use Linux operating system, but the security software and settings available to that Linux operating system are not used, installed, or running in an effort to still keep the operating system as lightweight on resources as possible. In doing so the space vehicle would be an extremely targetable and familiar target to malicious cyber actors. As developmental decisions to modernize are made, they need to be full implementations of modern solutions to include the security functions that can be utilized with them.

The Failure Analysis Problem

As the software definition of space vehicle (SV) components expands and the reliance of SVs on digital components increases, the threats posed by cyber attack are essentially innumerous and their potential impact immeasurable. The space industry has a robust failure analysis heritage; however, a purposeful cyber effect being the cause of a SV failure is likely to be overlooked for some time. This is due to the fact that an attacker skilled enough to gain access to the SV is likely capable of covering their tracks well and that the operators will focus on a failure analysis of what is known to them first. They will first ask questions of why did this component potentially physically fail? Then they will ask last if at all, did someone use a cyber attack to damage the SV? Until failure analysis begins with the cyber aspects such as the C&DH which ties all operations of the SV together or other integral components like SDRs, we will be actively losing ground to cyber attackers.

Conclusion

In conclusion I hope that this book has been educational to both cybersecurity professionals and any of those from the space industry or others that read it. To me the space domain is a really interesting and complex puzzle for cybersecurity, and I think that both industries need to embrace that they are inextricably tied. With the growth of the space industry and the overall increasing accessibility of space systems, the cybersecurity industry needs to understand the constraints and challenges of space operation.

In doing so we will be able to offer solutions that can be implemented in that unique environment that still allow space systems to accomplish their mission and not simply be another added constraint. The space industry needs to begin accepting that many of the threats to their systems while not cyber in nature can be brought about via cyber means. As the software definition of onboard functions increases, so too will the breadth of threats that a cyber attack could bring to bear on a space system.

Accepting that cybersecurity is a targeted and evolving risk to many aspects of space system operations is a must. Those responsible for space systems should go so far as at least taking a moment to ask the question, of any space system component having an issue, is this something that could be tied to a cyber attack, and has my space system been compromised? My hope in writing this book is that the scenarios of ships' computers being used to terrorize and attack the crew on board or other space vehicles remain in my beloved science fiction franchises and stay out of reality.

Index

© Jacob G. Oakley 2020
J. G. Oakley, *Cybersecurity for Space*, https://doi.org/10.1007/978-1-4842-5732-6

P, Q, R

S

Printed in the United States
By Bookmasters